Avengers and Defenders

AVENGERS AND DEFENDERS:
Glimpses of Chicago's Jewish Past

WALTER ROTH

Published in 2008 by
Academy Chicago Publishers
363 West Erie Street
Chicago, Illinois 60654

Published in association with
The Chicago Jewish Historical Society.

Printed in the USA

**Library of Congress Cataloging-in-Publication Data
on file with the publisher**

To my wife Chaya,
our children and grandchildren
and
my friends and colleagues of the
Chicago Jewish Historical Society

Contents

Part IV
SCIENCE IN THE CITY

Part V
AVENGERS AND DEFENDERS

Part VI
LOVERS OF ZION

Part VII
ADDENDA: AUTHOR'S MESSAGES TO THE CHICAGO JEWISH HISTORICAL SOCIETY 2003–2007

Acknowledgments

This book, *Avengers and Defenders: Glimpses of Chicago's Jewish Past* is a continuation of the anthology of my book, *Looking Backward: Stories from Chicago's Jewish Past*, published in 2002. Like *Looking Backward* the stories contained in this book were first written for the quarterly, Chicago Jewish History, published by the Chicago Jewish Historical Society. The present book carries the title of *Avengers and Defenders* because the stories included in this book deal with people who fought for their rights whether in politics or business often with great success. The first story involves the Haymarket riot that occurred over one hundred twenty five years ago, and while it may not have Jews, it had a lasting impact on the Jewish community. Another story deals with Sholom Schwartzbard who came to Chicago to tell his story of revenge when he assassinated the Crimean "Butcher." Then there is the story of Paley who defended Ed Murrow against McCarthy's attacks. Martin Kamen's story is included because he defended himself against libelous attacks by the Chicago Tribune who accused this Chicago scientist of being a Communist spy. He sued the *Tribune* and, against all odds, he won.

A number of stories deal with heroics in business ventures, and a number of others include persons of stature who achieved great success in law and academia. These are only a few examples of the brave avengers and defenders included in this volume.

The book concludes with an addendum recording some of the messages I wrote for our quarterly concerning my personal views and experiences that occurred from 2003 to the present.

My work relies heavily on the research sources of the Spertus Library, Newberry Library and Chicago History Museum.

Special thanks go to Bev Chubat, the editor of Chicago Jewish History Quarterly, who was of invaluable help in editing the original versions of my stories. I would like to thank Norman Schwartz, Adele Hast, Charles Bernstein, and Dan Sharon, members of our Society, for their research assistance, and Colleen Russell for her outstanding work.

I extend my gratitude to Anita and Jordan Miller of Academy Chicago Publishers and to Sarah Olson for her first rate production of this book.

Part I

Trouble in the City

1

Jewish Connections to the Haymarket Bomb Tragedy

On May 1, 1886, many of Chicago's workers went on a general strike in support of the eight-hour work day. Two days later, on May 3, the Chicago police fired into a crowd of strikers at the McCormick Reaper Works (later International Harvester) killing and wounding several strikers. That evening leaflets (many in German because of the large number of Germans in the labor force) were distributed by several anarchist groups calling for a protest meeting the next day near Haymarket Square.

At that time Haymarket Square was located on a widened portion of Randolph Street between DesPlaines and Halsted Streets. Despite dire predictions by the city's newspapers and police, the meeting proceeded without incident. In fact, Chicago's mayor, Carter H. Harrison Sr., was there mixing with the workers in the square. As the sky darkened into rainy twilight, Mayor Harrison and many of the crowd began to leave.

The last speaker, Samuel Fielden, was finishing his speech when a contingent of police marched into the square against Mayor Harrison's express orders to the captain in charge that no such action was needed. As the police captain ordered Fielden to end his speech, an explosive was thrown into the police ranks. Instantly the square was filled with a fuselage of retaliatory pistol fire from the police. Many in the crowd were killed and wounded. Sixty-seven policemen were hurt, eight of whom later died. It has since been established that most of the police casualties were caused by panic firing from the police themselves.

Eight men who had been leaders of various local anarchist groups were brought to trial for the bombing and the killing of a police officer, even though none of them was accused of actually throwing the lethal object. The bomb-thrower was never apprehended. The trial, amidst great drama and tension, lasted over a month, 21 days of which were taken to pick a jury.

The trial judge, Joseph E. Gary, ruled that the prosecution had only to demonstrate that the men on trial had conspired in speeches and writings to overthrow the law by force. If the policeman was killed in pursuance of such a conspiracy, the defendants were guilty of murder, even if none of them threw the bomb. The jury took only three hours to decide that the eight defendants were "accessories before the fact" and thus guilty of the murder of one of the slain policemen.

On November 11, 1887, four of the anarchists, Albert R. Parsons, August Spies, Adolph Fisher and George Engel, were hanged and later buried at Waldheim Cemetery. A fifth, Louis Lingg, either was murdered or committed suicide in his cell the day before the hangings when a dynamite cap detonated in his mouth. Six years later, in 1893, the three surviving anarchists were pardoned by Governor John Peter Altgeld.

A monument was erected at the Waldheim graveside of the four anarchists where heavily attended annual memorial services were held for years afterwards. The monument bears the inscription of the words uttered by August Spies as he stood on the scaffold: "The Day Will Come When Our Silence Will Be More Powerful Than The Voices You Are Throttling Today."

In his pardon, Governor Altgeld delivered a vehement attack on Judge Gary, accusing him of "malicious ferocity," maintaining that there was no evidence that any of the eight anarchists had been involved in the bombing. As a result, Altgeld came under vicious attacks from Chicago's press and business community. For his courageous action, the governor became an "Eagle Forgotten" (as the poet Vachel Lindsay called him); he was driven from office and his political career ruined. But when Altgeld died in 1902, his body lay in state in the Chicago Public Library, and tens of thousands of people waited in line on Michigan Avenue to pay their respects to him.

None of the convicted anarchists was Jewish. Parsons was a native-born American whose brother had been a general in the Confederate army. Samuel Fielden, one of the defendants who was pardoned, was born in Lancashire, England. The others were born in Germany, except for one, Dexter Neebe, who was born in New York but grew up in Germany. Indeed, there is some evidence that at least one of the defendants had expressed hostility to Jews, who were then beginning to arrive from Eastern Europe in increasing numbers, although the mass Eastern European Jewish immigration to Chicago was still some ten years away.

In 1886 it was Germans who led the anarchist movements in Chicago, and so it was Germans who were arrested. In later years, Jews were often identified with the "anarchists," and the term "anarchist" often became a code word for a "crazed immigrant," "labor agitator" or "socialist." But in 1886, when Chicago was in the grip of strikes and demonstrations, Jews were not involved with the anarchists in any meaningful way.

The set-up of the Amalgamated Clothing Workers Union and the Hart, Schaffner & Marx strike, in which many Jews were involved, did not occur until twenty years later. And at that time, most of the Jewish labor leaders in Chicago were socialists rather than anarchists, even though the Chicago newspapers found it difficult to draw a distinction between the two. Thus the Haymarket affair increased the tensions. Government and newspapers often confused union organization with anarchist activity. New immigrants became more suspect and Jewish immigrants to Chicago often found an "unwelcome" mat in many quarters.

Of course, some Jews did embrace the anarchist cause. Emma Goldman, a recent Jewish immigrant aged seventeen at the time of the Haymarket blast, later claimed that when she heard of the Haymarket hangings, she decided to become an anarchist. While Goldman did not live in Chicago, she often came to the city in the early 1900's to meet with her fellow anarchists and to struggle with the police. In her writings, she notes that she often stayed at the home of Dr. Miriam Yampolsky of the Edelstadt Lodge, an anarchist club. Dr. Yampolsky, a graduate of the University of Illinois, was a Jewish phyician.

Two Jewish lawyers did become involved in the Haymarket trial. The Chicago Central Labor Committee retained its attorney, Moses Salomon, and his associate Sigmund Zeisler, to defend the anarchists. As both were young, and Zeisler very inexperienced, a defense committee organized by the friends and family of the defendants, after much difficulty, retained older and more experienced gentile attorneys to lead the defense. They were Captain William Perkins Black, a liberal corporation lawyer, and William A. Foster, a criminal lawyer from Iowa.

After the trial, Black became a passionate advocate for the release of the defendants, but his legal career in later years was basically destroyed by the vicious attacks on him by the city's newspapers. Salomon participated actively in the trial and made one of the closing arguments for the defense. After the trial he seems to have disappeared from view. We do know that he was born in Peoria, Illinois, on December 13, 1857 and that in 1863 his Germaan Jewish family moved to Chicago. Salomon graduated from the Union College of Law in October, 1881. Sigmund Ziesler, the other Jewish lawyer, remained very much on the scene.

Many years later, on May 3, 1926, on the eve of the fortieth anniversary of the Haymarket bombing, Zeisler delivered a speech at the Chicago Literary Club recounting his recollections of the case and his conclusion that there was no evidence to convict the defendants. His speech was later printed in a book titled *Reminiscences of the Anarchist Case*.

Zeisler was the sole survivor of the trial; everyone else involved was dead: the presiding judge, the twelve jurors, the counsel for the state, the counsel for the defense (except himself), the police officials active in the trial, the nine justices of the United States Supreme Court, who were appealed to for a writ of error but had declined to act, and all the defendants. Zeisler was the only person clearly able to overcome the anarchist "taint." Indeed, he came to play an important role in the legal fraternity and in local Jewish society.

Born in Bielitz, Silesia, in 1860, Zeisler studied law in Vienna. He came to Chicago in 1883 and received a law degree from Northwestern University Law School in 1884. Two years later he participated in the anarchist trial. After the trial, he entered private practice and was a partner for a number of years of Julian W. Mack from San Francisco who was destined to become a famous judge, and Zack Hofheimer, originally from Virginia. Zeisler handled court appearances for the firm.

From 1904 to 1920 he was a master in chancery in the Circuit Court of Cook County, lectured on Roman law at Northwestern and constitutional law at John Marshall Law School. He was noted as a public speaker and was active in many civic and Jewish organisations. He died in 1931. His wife, Fannie Bloomfield Zeisler, was a celebrated pianist.

* * * *

On Memorial Day, 1889, a group of Chicago businessmen dedicated an imposing bronze statute in the Haymarket of a policeman with his right arm raised commanding peace. The model for the statue, Patrolman Thomas J. Birmingham, was then stationed in the Haymarket. A few years later he was dismissed from the force in disgrace, and died in 1912 on Skid Row. The statue itself was blown up several times during the anti-war demonstrations of the late 1960's. It was restored and today stands in the lobby of Chicago police headquarters. It undoubtedly is a fitting reminder of the violence which occurred in Chicago in 1886 and which is, too often, with us today.

2

The Peoria Street Riots of November 1949

In my "President's Column" in the Spring 2003 issue of *Chicago Jewish History*, I mentioned that Dan Sharon, Senior Research Librarian at the Asher Library, Spertus Institute of Jewish Studies, had brought to my attention the racial and anti-Semitic riots that occurred in November, 1949 in Englewood on Chicago's South Side. These riots followed similar disturbances in the Chicago area in the post-World War II years. They are worth examining now in light of anti-Semitic acts taking place around the world today. The following article is based on reportage, editorials, and articles on the Peoria Street events that appeared at the time in the Chicago daily newspapers, the Jewish weekly *Sentinel*, and several monthly magazines.

Mike Hecht, a young Chicago journalist, was an eyewitness to the events. He described them in an article, "Civil Rights on Peoria Street," in the February 1950 issue of *The Jewish Frontier*, a publication of the Labor Zionist movement.

"The outlines of the story are simple enough. Two young Jewish war veterans, friends for many years, tired of living in crumbling flats and dingy one-room apartments, saved a few dollars, pooled their resources, and purchased a 2-story building at 5643 S. Peoria Street, in Englewood, a residential area on Chicago's

Southwest Side. In October, Bill Sennett, his wife Gussie and their little daughters, ages 8 and 4, moved in to the upstairs apartment; two weeks later, Aaron Bindman, and his wife Louise moved in downstairs."

Their new home was located near a Catholic Church—the Visitation Parish Church—on the corner of Peoria and 55th Street (Garfield Boulevard), where "the Monsignor preached a sermon requesting good Christians not to sell their homes to 'undesirables'. . ."

On Tuesday evening, November 8, 1949, Bindman held a reception in his apartment for union members. Eight of the invited guests were black. As if by pre-arrangement, an alarm was sounded that Negroes had purchased the house and a mob of "minutemen" assembled, shouting insults against Jews and Negroes. Wednesday morning, Bindman and some friends called on Chicago's Police Commissioner John Pendergast and other police officials for protection; all were unavailable. A visit to Mayor Martin Kennelly's office proved similarly fruitless.

By Wednesday night, a crowd of hundreds gathered around the Bindman-Sennet house; the three policemen assigned to guard the house made no attempt to disperse them. Maynard Wishner, a member of the Mayor's Commission on Human Relations, contacted the Englewood Police and was told by an officer that "everything was all right" and it was difficult to disperse the crowd because they were neighbors—but a fourth policeman was assigned to protect Bindman's home. According to Mike Hecht, by Thursday morning, the whole neighborhood knew that Negroes had not bought the house and that the Bindman and Sennett families did not intend to sell their house.

About 8:30 p.m. on Wednesday, the crowd stormed the Bindman porch, shouting "Let's go in and kill the Jews." The few policemen at the scene asked them to stop, and soon about 20 additional policemen arrived. The crowd, now constantly increasing in size, began to hurl stones and rocks at the home, shattering windows and causing other damage. The police did nothing to prevent this violence. Some of Bindman's friends attempted to come to his assistance, but they were beaten, as were other persons who were strangers to the crowd. The police finally arrested two rock-throwers as well as two friends of Bindman. Taken to the police station, Bindman's friends were booked but the rock-throwers were released.

The mob grew through the night. By some counts over 2,500 people surrounded the house, with hundreds of others in nearby streets. Many persons were beaten, some seriously, including several University of Chicago students and a *Chicago Daily News* reporter. The police did not interfere with the activities of the crowd. An editorial in the *Daily News* complained that the police were almost provocative in their hostility to Bindman. A policeman had stated to the paper's reporter that the victims were properly beaten because they were Communists. "How do you know they were Communists?" the reporter inquired. "Because they were Jews," the policeman replied.

Hecht also notes that mobs roamed the business district near Peoria Street, smashing windows of Jewish-owned stores and attacking anyone they thought to be Jewish. Blacks did not dare to walk in the area.

The Chicago press finally took up the story in greater detail. Editorials in the *Daily News* and the *Sun-Times* called attention to the events, and launched an attack on Mayor Kennelly for his inaction during the week of rioting. The Mayor, now also facing mounting criticism from various Jewish organizations, including Jewish veterans' groups, as well as the American Civil Liberties Union, finally issued an order to the Chicago police to restore order in Englewood.

Mike Hecht concludes: "Such are the bare facts and the broad outlines: 'A man's home is his castle' is accepted as gospel, a man invites into his home friends and colleagues for a peaceful gathering; his neighbors form a mob, which begins by shouting anti-Negro epithets, and winds up with a full scale three-day pogrom against Jews and 'strangers,' bragging that it will finish what Hitler left undone; the mob is instigated and organized by substantial interests; the police stand by permitting the violence to develop and flare, and in numerous cases, encourage and provoke the violence, while the Mayor and the police commissioner are too occupied to intervene, and newspapers have no space to report the event. People in Chicago are wondering about the state of civil rights."

Within a week after the Peoria Street riots, the Chicago Jewish weekly *Sentinel*, in its November 24, 1949 issue, carried a letter from Edgar Bernhard, an attorney and officer of the American Civil Liberties Union, to Mayor Kennelly summarizing the events from the ACLU's viewpoint:

> I consider it my duty to report to you the deep disappointment in many quarters as the result of your handling of the recent outbreak of anti-Negro and anti-Semitic violence at 56th and South Peoria Streets Tuesday night, November 8. During your administration there has been a series of outbreaks of violence against Chicago citizens because of their racial, religious or ethnic origins. You have had at your disposal not only the entire police force of the City but the support of the City Commission on Human Relations and the support of numerous civic and church organizations interested in human relations, including the Chicago Division of the American Civil Liberties Union. The latter organizations have repeatedly brought to your attention the seriousness of these outbreaks and made constructive suggestions as to dealing with them. Delay, failure to speak out, and waiting to see whether the situation will not perhaps take care of itself have sometimes intensified situations and increased risks and dangers which would have been at least allayed by forthright statements and decisive action by you at the inception of each such outbreak.
>
> Eyewitness investigators, who have reported to us, have told appalling stories of human beings beaten and trampled upon; of the gathering of a crowd of over two hundred people with only

three policemen on hand, and later of the gathering of several hundred more people with only twenty policemen on hand; of the fact that the policemen were speaking pleasantly to people in the mob and mildly asking, "Why don't you go home?" instead of seeing to it that the crowds were dispersed; of the throwing of stones by the crowd—and still no dispersal; of physical attacks on people who happened to be walking in the neighborhood, some of whom did not even know what the crowd were gathered for; and of police being forced back by the crowd instead of the crowd being forced back by the police!

You have been asked on a number of occasions by responsible people representing organizations whose membership includes several hundred thousand Chicagoans to issue a statement which would once and for all make it plain that the policy of the City Administration not only does not condone the violation of law and order but stands ready and able to enforce the laws of this city, the State of Illinois, and the Nation, which laws can be interpreted in no other way than to grant to all persons, regardless of race, religion or ethnic origin, the right to rent, buy, live and travel in any part of the city. Your attention has been called to rumors, which have been heard repeatedly from those engaged in mob violence, that you personally and your administration do not believe in upholding these laws and protecting the civil rights of minority group members who exercise these rights by moving into property which they own or have rented in areas previously established in the minds of some people as 'pure white.'

As reported by the Press, you have finally, as of Friday, made a public statement . . . In your statement, you made mention of "subversive groups and individuals who thrive on disorder". In view of police attitudes openly expressed during the 56th and Peoria violence, it is necessary for me to point out that it is the responsibility of city officials to protect the civil rights and persons of all the people, no matter who they are, where they come from or what any individual policeman may think of them.

Rabbi Morton M. Berman, President of both the Chicago Division of the American Jewish Congress, and of the Chicago Rabbinical Association, also wrote a letter to Kennelly:

> Newspaper editorials have already pointed out the police's failure and indeed their acquiescence in some of the mob action. You, Mr. Mayor, refused to take any forthright public position despite full knowledge of what was happening and of Chicago's experience with similar incidents receiving nationwide attention during your term of office. Your vague statement calling for law and order issued a week after violence had ended will not convince anyone that he risks serious punishment if he resorts to violence to interfere with anyone's right to live or visit where he pleases.

On December 1, 1949, the *Sentinel* carried an angry editorial by its editor Jack Fishbein attacking Mayor Kennelly for his mishandling of the Peoria riots. After reciting his complaints, Fishbein concludes: "And where is the conscience of Chicago Jewry? Silent . . . silent as the graves of the six million Jews who sleep their silent sleep in Buchenwald and Dachau and Treblinka."

A less dramatic discussion of the Peoria violence was carried several weeks later in the January 2, 1950, issue of the *Congress Weekly*, the official organ of the American Jewish Congress, in an article written by attorney Byron S. Miller, AJC's Midwest Director of the Commission on Law and Social Action. Recounting much of the material detailed by Hecht, Miller recalls that in the same week as the Peoria Street riot, similar mob action had begun in the neighboring Park Manor area, where there had been a prior major racial riot and "innumerable" incidents of attacks on Negro families who had tried to move into that area. But there the police had moved promptly to put up barricades and disperse onlookers, avoiding further violence.

The same officer who had succeeded in handling the Park Manor outbreak was apparently (by lucky chance) brought over to

Peoria Street on Saturday night, five days after the initial outbreak of mob action on Peoria Street. Using similar tactics, this officer and the police were able to quickly disperse the crowd in Peoria Street neighborhoods and "the area has been orderly since then."

Miller writes that this action came in the nick of time because "militant members of the Negro community" had decided to take matters in their own hands and to set out for Peoria Street to retaliate. If the crowd had not already been dispersed, Miller writes, Chicago might have had another lethal race riot on its hands, reminiscent of the murderous Chicago race riots of the summer of 1919. As it was, this was avoided, though Miller points out that it was a very narrow escape. A civil libertarian, Miller spells out the need for community awareness and organization. He recalls that a citizen group, the Chicago Council Against Racial and Religious Discrimination, met with the Mayor and pressured him to issue orders to implement police procedures designed to produce the "kind of trained and disinterested policemen who would enforce the words contained in these orders." Effective police protection would be the result.

By the time Miller was writing his article, almost two months after the riots, Peoria Street was quiet and the first Negro family was moving in. Miller writes that racial tensions remained high, and whites were fleeing the neighborhood, selling their homes at distressed prices. "If the whites would only stay and not see the Negroes as a violent threat to their safety, prices would not be depressed and whites would stay. Once this attitude is achieved, violence of the Chicago pattern will be a thing of the past."

Miller could still hope for this result in January 1950. But as whites moved out, Englewood soon turned into an almost entirely black neighborhood. Racial violence continued on Chicago's Southwest side, climaxing in the Marquette riots during Martin Luther King's integration efforts in the 1960's. The struggle exemplified by the Peoria Street riots of November 1949 should be a constant reminder of the ever present danger of uncontrolled mob action, the need for leadership in our community, and the protection that must be made available to all citizens, no matter what their race, religion or ethnic origin.

3

Meyer Levin and the Memorial Day Massacre of 1937

Meyer Levin's novel *The Old Bunch*, published in 1937, deals with the lives of a group of Jewish teenagers from Chicago's West Side as they grow to adulthood. Some of the characters are idealists who become doctors, public school teachers, and participants in the labor union turmoil of the Depression years. The book, at 964 pages, Levin called his "magnum opus."

Levin himself became involved in the seething labor strife involving the workers in steel mills in the Chicago area. At the time he had joined an organization called "New America." In his autobiography *In Search* (Horizon Press, New York, 1950), Levin refers to "New America" as typical of a score of organizations on Chicago's West Side that "attracted non-communist progressives. . . ." To him, it was an advocacy group for a "Super New Deal." Through New America, intellectuals like Levin were apparently seeking to become union organizers for the CIO (Congress of Industrial Workers Organization).

A large protest demonstration by the CIO and their sympathizers, seeking their right to organize, occurred on the afternoon of Memorial Day, May 30, 1937, in a field near the Republic Steel plant in South East Chicago. As a freelance reporter, Levin saw this confrontation between the workers and their employer as the basis of a novel he had in mind and which he would call *Citizens*. Levin attended the demonstration and joined the crowd on Memorial Day. What transpired that day has been documented by the Illinois Labor History Society in a video containing actual footage of the demonstration. An article from the Illinois Labor History Society web site reads:

> Ten demonstrators were killed by police bullets during the "Little Steel Strike of 1937" which occurred on May 30th of that year. When several smaller steelmakers, including Republic Steel, refused to follow the lead of U.S. Steel ("Big Steel") by signing a union contract, a strike was called by the Steel Workers Organizing Committee (SWOC) of the CIO. To show support, hundreds of SWOC sympathizers from all around Chicago gathered on Memorial Day at Sam's Place, where the SWOC had its strike headquarters. After a routine round of speeches, the crowd began a march across the prairie toward the Republic Steel mill. They were stopped midway by a formation of Chicago police. While demonstrators in front were arguing for their right to proceed, police fired into the crowd and pursued the people who fled. Mollie West, a Typographical Union Local 16 member and a youthful demonstrator at the time, still recalls the command addressed to her: "Get off the field or I'll put a bullet in your back."

Mollie West is now executive secretary of the Illinois Labor History Society. She with many other Jewish union members or sympathizers had driven to the Memorial Day demonstration to show their solidarity with the steelworkers. She is now in her late eighties and still recalls the speech she made at the time on behalf of the strikers. She also recalls that a dance scheduled that night at the Jewish People's Institute on the West Side was cancelled and turned into a rally for the workers killed and wounded in what would later be called "The Memorial Day Massacre of 1937."

Many members from other unions joined the Memorial Day

demonstration, including unions that were predominantly Jewish. For example, Leo Krzyeki, an Amalgamated Clothing Worker's Union organizer of the Chicago-Milwaukee region, spoke to the crowd praising President Roosevelt and supporting the workers' right to organize.

Meyer Levin saw everything that happned: the speeches, the shootings and the chaos that followed, and recorded his interviews and notes for his novel. He went to the hospital where he saw and photographed the ten dead and seventy-five wounded, who included women and children.

A Senate Committee chaired by Senator Robert LaFollette of Wisconsin sent investigators to Chicago and then held meetings in Washington. While most of the Chicago press (particularly the *Chicago Tribune*) condemned the strikers as "Reds" and accused them of instigating the attack, the LaFollette Committee blamed the Republic Steel plant management and the Chicago Police. Chicago Mayor Edward J. Kelly promised that no such event would ever occur again in Chicago.

Levin, in his autobiography, reports on the "Jew-baiting" and "Fascistic" reaction of the police, but took comfort in the mass rally held the following week, on June 8, 1937, at the Chicago Opera House, in support of the strikers and as a memorial to the victims. Paul Douglas, professor at the University of Chicago, was chairman of the rally, and would later be elected U.S. Senator from Illinois.

Levin was not yet ready to sit down to work on his Chicago labor union novel, *Citizens*. Instead, he sought out another "hot" reportorial assignment, this time far away from Chicago. He approached the publisher Melvin Morris, who was establishing a new "liberal" magazine called *Inside*, and obtained an assignment to report on the raging Spanish Civil War. Levin went to Spain in the summer of 1937, one month after the labor strike, to gather material dealing with the Spanish Civil War. His wife accompanied him to Spain. She became pregnant there, and a son, Eli, now an artist living in Santa Fe, New Mexico, was born.

Levin wrote about the Spanish Civil War without much probing or analysis. He simply found that the "Left" was losing to the "Fascistic" forces of the "Right." Levin was at a loss to explain the discord among the Anarchists, Communists and Socialists, in this conflict with the Franco forces. A few months later, strangely and without explanation once again, he decided to leave Spain and went to Palestine for the third time. He wrote then that the same "Fascistic" forces that he encountered in Spain were the cause of the riots that were engulfing much of Palestine, a highly debatable view. He met old friends from his former trips to Palestine and found himself with people with whom he could identify.

Nevertheless, with war breaking out in Europe in September 1939, and with the birth of his son, Levin returned to the United States to begin writing *Citizens*, his version of the "Little Steel" strike. As with some of his earlier novels, Levin wrote this one as a "social realist" studying the socio-political situation in America. While none of his earlier novels had been commercially successful and despite a "writer's block," to which he alluded a number of times, Levin was determined to proceed with his "strike" novel.

He rented a room in Gary, Indiana, near the steel mills, where he managed to get hired to do some administrative work at one of the nearby steel mills, so that he could meet the workers, learn about the their various jobs, talk with them about their lives, their hopes and dreams, and fears. Most of all, he could learn about the workers' relationship to the economic system and to the class struggle he saw taking place in America. He would follow the work in the mill of each of the ten workers killed in the strike so "that each portion of the novel furthered the other."

Levin used testimony from the Senate hearings and from his own notes to relate actual events, but also added fiction to shape the narrative as he wanted it told about the working class. About a hundred pages of *Citizens* deal with the actual strike story; the rest of the book is about the lives of the slain strikers; many of the lives he described were in fact a composite of a number of persons.

As with Levin himself at the time, his characters are alienated and consider themselves society's outsiders, unable to become part of a cohesive, creative group in America.

There were no Jewish figures in this novel, except for Mitch Wilner, the young doctor who is a leading character in *The Old Bunch*. Wilner who witnessed the killings that took place during the course of the strike, became Levin's main narrator. Levin used Wilner as the device to question workers, to talk with them and to tell their side of the "class struggle": the violence and bias of the police and the suffering of the workers and their families. The police are not treated with sympathy. Of the few policemen depicted individually, one is the "bull cop," a man of violence, and others appear as victims of circumstances, deliberately whipped into a frenzy by their evil superiors.

One cannot help but conclude that Levin, at least in this 1940 novel, saw the workers as the victims of a capitalistic system which controlled their destiny. Despite this, he protested often in his writings at the time, that he was not a communist, that he hated communism for its complete control of the individual citizen in society.

The novel is a successful portrayal of human suffering and social conflict. As in Levin's own personal life at the time, his characters were often alienated, considered themselves to be society's outsiders and were unable to become part of a cohesive creative group in America.

Levin could not deal with the problems he so astutely observed in a manner that would satisfy his readers, and his book *Citizens* reflects a general malaise affecting Jewish writers striving to become part of the general American literary scene. It would take more than two decades before Bernard Malamud, Saul Bellow and Phillip Roth became successful Jewish writers in America.

After he had finished a draft of *Citizens* in the fall of 1939, Levin went to New York to confer with his publisher who "could see my book as a really outstanding American novel—a sort of industrial *Grapes of Wrath* and was prepared to launch it as such." The publisher had one main objection—it concerned Mitch Wilner, the Jewish doctor who helped the strikers. He wanted the doctor to be more typically American, perhaps of Northern European descent. Levin objected; not only was Wilner a link to *The Old Bunch*, but Levin knew, as he writes in his autobiography, any doctor moving in labor circles would most likely be Jewish. As for being typical of the American scene: "since my book followed a set of actual events, it would be a distortion to pretend that the doctor was not a Jew."

Levin thought about the publisher's suggestion, had a dream about it, agonized about it, and then informed his publisher that he "could not alter the Wilner character." "There had to be a world in which honesty was permissible." So the Jewish Dr. Wilner, remained the main character in the novel, which was published by Viking Press in 1940, just as Levin had originally written it.

With the exception of his novel *Compulsion* (1966), *Citizens* was the last book Levin wrote about the American scene. He turned away from his struggle with his identity as a Jew in America, as well as from the socio-political problems of this country. His experiences as a reporter in World War II Europe (1942–1945), and as an early eyewitness to the horrors of the death camps changed the direction of Levin's life and work. He married again, this time a young Frenchwoman, Tereska, who was a survivor of the Holocaust and a Zionist, and began writing on distinctly Jewish themes and with a Zionist outlook.

But life did not become easier for him, and his struggles continued with his new works. Controversy and litigation over his "Jewish-Zionist" dramatization of *The Diary of Anne Frank* lasted almost a decade. Moreover, his most successful book, play and movie, *Compulsion,* involved him in another ten-year court battle in Illinois.

On Sunday, May 30, 2004, at 3:00 p.m. at the Union Memorial Hall, 11731 South Avenue O, Chicago, a commemoration of the

"Memorial Day Massacre of 1937" was held. One of the speakers, Ed Sadlowski, a former district director of the Steelworkers' Union said: "We are holding this memorial because we are proud of our heritage. We want to inform our children and our children's children, that all the gains we have made we owe to those who stood and died on the field that day." Meyer Levin would have agreed. Although *Citizens* was not a commercial success, Sadlowski, now a teacher of History at Indiana State University, uses Levin's novel as a textbook in his classroom, a textbook about the "Memorial Day Massacre of 1937."

4

Levy Mayer and the Iroquois Theatre Fire

One century ago in Chicago, on the afternoon of December 30, 1903, there occurred a horrific event at the Iroquois Theatre, located on Randolph Street between State and Dearborn, where the Oriental Theater now stands—refurbished and renamed Ford Center for the Performing Arts. In less than 20 minutes, over 600 persons, mostly children and women, died in a catastrophic fire that engulfed the theatre.

A recent book, *Tinder Box*, by Anthony P. Hatch (Academy Chicago Publishers 2003) recalls, in personal interviews and collections of stories of survivors, the traumatic terror these people endured when fire engulfed the theatre. In the audience were people from all parts of the city. A number of gravestones in Jewish cemeteries record that the child "died during the Iroquois fire." It was Chicago's worst fire up to that time and since then, far exceeding the casualties resulting from the great Chicago fires of 1871 and 1874.

An ominous atmosphere quickly developed after the fire. Rage seized Chicago's populace, constantly fanned by newspaper accounts of the tragedy. The feeling was that somebody was responsible and whoever it was must be punished! Reporters quickly discovered that recently enacted city ordinances had not been complied with: the sprinkler system did not work, the doors only opened toward the inside, exit signs were missing, the skylight could not be opened, among many other violations. Within a few days, the theatre manager and other employees were arrested for manslaughter, and a number of persons, including the mayor, Carter H. Harrison, were held for action by a grand jury.

Among the cast of characters whose names now became known to the public were Marc Klaw and Abraham Lincoln Erlanger. These men, with other partners, controlled the Theatrical Trust, which from its offices on Broadway in New York City, held a virtual monopoly of many legitimate theaters in America, including the Iroquois. The Trust owned the theaters and also controlled the bookings and ticket prices—which aroused great antagonism. Leading clergymen of the day, together with the press and independent theater owners, held the Trust "responsible for the degradation of the American theatre" and the corruption of "Christian morals."

As Hatch writes, "It was easy to dislike Marc Klaw and Abe Erlanger. And they were Jews." With thousands of poor Russian Jewish immigrants streaming into the city, coupled with their strange Yiddish language, dress and customs, anti-Semitism was rife in the city. The legacy of the Haymarket Riot and anarchist scares still existed, spurred on by media sensationalism.

Klaw and Erlanger were in financial trouble in 1903 and, with the Trust, were involved in bitter labor disputes. Chicago was in the midst of a transit strike and there were daily stories of crime and corruption. The Iroquois was slated to open in November and Klaw and Erlanger allegedly cut costs in order to meet the opening date. It was said that such items as the fireproof curtains and firefighting equipment were not up to standard because of the need to cut expenses. The play scheduled to be produced by Klaw and Erlanger was a musical comedy called *Mr. Bluebeard*, starring Eddie Foy, with music by Frederick Soloman and Herbert Kerr. It was during a holiday matinee performance of *Mr. Bluebeard*, before an audience composed largely of children, that the fire broke out.

The Klaw-Erlanger organization was attacked for disregarding the safety of its patrons by violating city fire regulations. *Life* magazine (no relation to the magazine of the same name which came into existence later) named Klaw and Erlanger in the caption of a cartoon showing the figure of Death blocking the way of the victims struggling to open the exit doors.

Initially the main target of critics like the *Chicago Tribune*, was Mayor Carter H. Harrison, because of his "indolent" behavior toward municipal corruption on every level of local government. He was held by the police for arraignment. However, within a week after his "retention" for a grand jury hearing, he was released on a writ of *habeas corpus*, since there was nothing to directly connect him with the operation of the Iroquois Theatre. "Let no man escape," one minister shouted as he viewed the gruesome theatre scene.

Rabbi Moses Peretz Jacobson of Kehilat Anshe Ma'ariv (K.A.M.), conducting the funeral for two Jewish children, called the fire "one of the great calamities of the age." Another rabbi at a memorial service was quoted as saying, "This fire was not an act of God but due to ignorance, criminal neglect and recklessness."

The inquest by the Coroner's Office began in City Hall on February 7, 1905, with over 200 witnesses called to testify. At the same time a "deluge of suits" was filed against the theatre, its management, owners and the City of Chicago. On January 25, the Coroner's verdicts were returned, naming Mayor Harrison, Iroquois Theatre Manager Will Davis, the City Building Commissioner and others. Klaw and Erlanger, though often mentioned in testimony as responsible for the faulty curtains and other violations, were not named.

The Grand Jury, after its secret deliberations, returned its indictments on February 23, naming Will Davis, Stage Manager James Cummings, and Business Manager James Noonan. The Jury exonerated Mayor Harrison, but said there "should be a more intelligent administrator in City Hall." The charge against the three indicted men was manslaughter.

In addition to the criminal charges, there were of course a host of civil suits against these and other defendants—among them Klaw and Erlanger, who lived in New York, which may have been one of the reasons why the Chicago Grand Jury did not reach them. Their own New York attorneys, deeply involved in the Iroquois cases, soon began to work closely with Levy Mayer, the attorney hired by the Chicago defendants.

Levy Mayer's parents had immigrated to the United States from small towns in Bavaria, Germany; Levy was born in 1858 in Richmond, Virginia. The Mayers relocated to Chicago where Levy attended public schools. In 1876 he graduated from Yale Law School. Too young to enter law practice, he started his legal career as researcher and librarian at the Chicago Law Institute. From there he was asked to become a partner by Adolf Kraus, a prominent attorney and leader of the Reform Jewish community.

The partnership, after a number of name changes, became in the early 1900s the respected firm of Mayer, Austrian & Platt, specializing in corporate, banking, government and international law. Levy Mayer was its dominant figure, with a reputation for brilliance and integrity. An imposing six feet tall, he had an enormous capacity to retain facts and cases, was said to speak clearly and was considered " a combative adversary."

It was reported that a day after the Iroquois fire, Klaw and Erlanger and their New York attorneys had asked Mayer to represent not only their interests but also the interests of others who might be indicted by the grand jury. Hatch, in his book *Tinderbox*, writes that Klaw and Erlanger, after a long meeting with executives of the Theatrical Trust, selected Mayer and his firm to head the defense team. Some have said that it took enormous courage for Mayer to take on this unpopular case.

Levy Mayer's legal brilliance was soon evident. He filed a motion to quash the charge against Theatre Manager Davis because the charge did not properly specify the legal duty to discharge the acts complained of in the indictment, and he filed a motion for a change of venue so that Business Manager Noonan and Stage Manager Cummings could get a "fair trial." This motion was granted and their case was moved to Peoria. On July 9, 1905, Mayer' strategy was marked with success, when the two judges in Peoria and Chicago quashed the charges on similar grounds, that there was no express duty binding the defendants. Mayer announced that "any future indictments would not be worth the paper they were written on."

Nevertheless, one month later, another Chicago Grand Jury indicted Will Davis and two others on manslaughter charges. Klaw and Erlanger were not indicated, on grounds of insufficient evidence. Mayer promptly filed a motion to quash and it was not until January 13, 1906, that the Davis indictment was sustained by the Illinois courts. As a trial date loomed, Mayer filed a motion for change of venue. In a brilliant stroke, he had many members of his staff collect over 12,000 affidavits attesting to bias and prejudice against the defendants.

The Davis trial was moved to Danville, a town over 100 miles south of Chicago. The trial began on March 7, 1907 and was expected to be lengthy. The prosecution was said to be prepared to call over 200 witnesses to testify. As the first witness, a woman dressed in black, was sworn in, Mayer rose to demand the state produce the Chicago City Ordinances on which the indictments were based. As this was done, Mayer filed a lengthy 231-page brief attacking the validity of the ordinances. As Hatch put it, as this was done, "the doors to the courtroom were flung open and a procession of bellboys and porters [entered] loaded down with piles of law books that they heaped on defense counsel's table." Mayer continued to argue his case before an enthralled audience and a curious Judge.

The essence of Mayer's argument, which the research supported, was that the ordinances were invalid because the State of

Illinois had not actually delegated to Chicago the power to enact its ordinances; this was before Home Rule was granted to the City of Chicago by the State legislature.

After a thirteen-hour presentation, Mayer concluded his case and moved for a directed verdict because the ordinances were not valid. The Judge agreed. Without the benefit of the ordinances, the Judge directed the jury to return a not-guilty verdict in the manslaughter case stating: "If it were in my power to bring back life and put the bloom of youth into the cheeks of these young girls by incarcerating the defendant in this case in the penitentiary for the term of his natural life, I would do it; but I cannot."

It had taken two-and-a-half years to conclude the trial. Mayer's strategy had earned him a prominent place in Chicago judicial history - though the results were sharply criticized by many, both in legal journals and media publications.

For the victims and their relatives there was now only the consolation that civil actions might be more successful. Numerous suits had been brought after the fire, but after the long delay it appeared that "most families of the dead and injured received not so much as a dime for compensation." Hatch reports that there were rumors that the Klaw-Erlanger organization eventually paid small amounts to relatives of the victims, but there was never any real evidence of that. In 1909, there was a report that the Fuller Construction Co. had paid $750 in thirty cases, but that over 400 cases were still pending. Since such suits are usually handled by plaintiffs' attorneys on a contingency basis, and since these attorneys knew they would be up against Levy Mayer in Chicago and other powerful Klaw-Erlanger lawyers in New York, it is doubtful that any litigation succeeded.

As for life insurance on the victims' lives, U.S. Judge Kenesaw Mountain Landis had ruled in a "theatre liability suit" that the Iroquois Theatre was not responsible for failure to comply with the Chicago ordinances providing for fire equipment on appliances of the Theatre. (Landis, incidentally, was the Judge who would become the first Commissioner of Major League Baseball following the "Black Sox" scandal. Landis was responsible for the expulsion of a number of Chicago White Sox players for allegedly "throwing" games in the 1919 World Series. The attorney representing Charles Comiskey, the owner of the White Sox, was Levy Mayer.)

The Iroquois Fire had enhanced Mayer's reputaion as one of Chicago's ablest attorneys, though not necessarily the most popular In a biography of him by Edgar Lee Masters, the author of *The Spoon River Anthology*, the details of the Iroquois Fire are amply covered, but other aspects of Mayer's life are not mentioned. There is not one mention of the fact that he was Jewish.

H.L. Meites, however, in his classic *History of Jews of Chicago* (Chicago Jewish Historical Society of Illinois, 1924) has a number of references to Mayer, including a summary of his life. In the chapter on leading Chicago Jewish lawyers, Meites also notes that Mayer served as Secretary of the Zion Literary Society, which was "the big cultural and social force in Chicago during the 1870s and 1880s, and held crowded meetings every Friday night at Zion Temple."

Meites also comments that Mayer attained nation-wide fame as a lawyer, "though with the passing of years, sad to state, he became estranged from Jewish efforts." But Meites does report that in 1916 Mayer was chairman of a large public fundraiser at the Auditorium Theatre to help Jews made destitute by World War I. Meites writes that the Auditorium gathering followed a dinner the night before at the home of Julius Rosenwald.

Levy Mayer died on August 14, 1922, some say from overwork. He was a workaholic, completely engrossed in his law practice up to the last day of his life. Since his wife and two daughters were away in Europe at the time of his death, the funeral service was not held until their return on August 24.

The memorial ceremony was at Sinai Temple, attended by a huge assemblage of leading personalities, particularly from the legal and business field. Abraham L. Erlanger of Iroquois Fire notoriety was there, and there were numerous eulogies.

He was interred in the family mausoleum at Rosehill Cemetery.

The Sentinel in its August 18, 1922 edition, carried a story under the headline "Levy Mayer, Noted Jewish Lawyer Dead." It noted that Mayer had made gifts to a number of Jewish charities in his lifetime. "His residence[s were] a palatial suite in the Blackstone Hotel [and] a summer home and large farm in Manomet, Mass. The fortune of Mr. Mayer is estimated at $25,000,000 . . ."

5

Frankie Foster: Did He Really Murder Jake Lingle?

Michael Karsen, a member of the Chicago Jewish Historical Society and a noted Chicago genealogist recently sent me an article written by a relative, Ira Eisenberg, published in the *San Jose Mercury News* on July 4, 1993 entitled "My uncle, the gangster." My interest was immediately caught by the article's opening paragraph:

> "The events occurred more than six decades ago, yet my 80 year-old mother remembers them as if they happened only yesterday. She was just a teen-ager in June 1930, living on Chicago's North Side and on her way home from school with some friends. 'We passed a newsstand and I saw the headline,' Mom recalls. 'It said, "Frankie Foster Indicted For Murder." I just left my girlfriends standing there and ran the rest of the way home.'
>
> Frankie Foster was my mother's older brother, the mysterious Uncle Frank I never knew, and about whom members of my family spoke only rarely and in cryptic terms. He had just been accused of a sensational crime, one that would expose Chicago's corrupt underbelly and shake up the city's power structure, the killing of Chicago Tribune reporter Jake Lingle."

Our Historical Society publications have carried several stories I have written about Chicago Jewish underworld characters such as "Nails" Morton and the Miller brothers. I knew about the Lingle case and the mysteries surrounding his murder, but here I learned for the first time that Frankie Foster, a Jew, was the alleged assassin of Jake Lingle. Despite advice from friends that this was a waste of my time, I decided to see what was behind this tale. To those of you unfamiliar with this "classic" murder, let me relate what some of my research disclosed.

Alfred "Jake" Lingle was an Irishman who worked for the *Chicago Tribune* for many years as a "leg man," meaning he called in his information to a rewrite man at the newspaper office, who then shaped it into a story for publication. (It was said of Lingle that he could not spell "cat"—but in those days a street reporter's most valuable assets were his contacts and confidentiality, not his writing skills). Over the years he appears to have established contacts with the various gangs that controlled the distribution of liquor, gambling, women and other illegal activities thriving in Chicago in the late 1920s.

While Lingle earned a respectable salary of $65 per week, he had a chauffeured limo, a fancy apartment and spent a great deal of money on the "ponies." He also appears to have had close contacts with his childhood friend, Chicago's Police Chief William P. Russell, Al Capone, the leader of the "South Side" gangs, as well as "Hymie" Weiss and George "Bugs" Moran, successors to Dino O'Banion, as leaders of the North Side Gangs.

Ever since the St. Valentine's Day Massacre in 1929 in which Capone's men allegedly murdered seven (7) of Moran's men in a North Clark Street garage, there were rumors that Lingle owed a great deal of money to Capone for losses on his gambling activities, and there were other rumors that he had attempted to extort money from Moran, who wanted to reopen his Sheridan Club, a large North side gambling hub which had been closed by the police in a crackdown after the St. Valentine's Day Massacre.

Enter Frankie Foster. A minor figure, he had been part of Dion O'Banion's gang, was a friend of "Nails" Morton and now seemingly working for "Bugs" Moran. In fact, it was thought that Frankie has been killed in the St. Valentine's Day Massacre, but the body first identified as his was someone else; Frankie escaped the killing. Between the time of the massacre and the Lingle murder, over 100 gang members were killed in the war between the North and the South Side gangs. The *Tribune* and its owner, Colonel McCormick, was one of the civic organizations calling for an end to this mayhem in the city.

On the morning of June 9, 1930, Lingle, cigar in mouth and *Racing Form* in hand, walked to the Randolph Street pedestrian underpass to catch an Illinois Central train to the Washington Park racetrack. As he walked through the tunnel, a gunman who had been following him pulled out a revolver and shot Lingle in the head, killing him. As the gunman turned to flee, two men dressed as Catholic priests, stepped between the escaping killer and people trying to catch him. Later it was suggested that the "priests" must have been part of the murder plot.

The Lingle murder caused sensational headlines in Lingle's newspaper, the *Chicago Tribune*, where rewards were advertised "totaling $55,725 for information leading to the arrest and conviction of the slayer of Alfred Lingle." On the day of his funeral, flags flew at half mast and brass bands and mourners paraded down Michigan Avenue following the hearse. It soon turned out that vast amounts of money were found on Lingle's body and in his safes and that he had been receiving all types of "favors" from illegal elements, in addition to other nefarious activities in which he was engaged. Needless to say, the *Tribune* was humiliated to discover that one of its own had been working with the gangs, since it had been a leader in the call for elimination of the mobs.

The Chicago police suspected Frankie of Lingle's murder. The ownership of the murder weapon, a .38 caliber revolver left at the scene of the crime, was traced to a Diversey Parkway retailer who had provided the machine guns used in the St. Valentine's Day Massacre. The serial number on the revolver, which had been partially filed off, led to Frankie as the purchaser of the revolver a number of years earlier. An order was issued for Frankie's arrest. He had vanished, but he was soon picked up in Los Angeles and extradited to Chicago where he was released after a hearing on the evidence.

The police arrested Ted Newberry, another Jew, because he was with Frankie when Frankie purchased the murder weapon, and was involved in some of the same "ventures" as Frankie. Newberry was also released, and was later killed by Capone. Also arrested was Julian "Potatoes" Kaufman, one of the owners of the Sheridan Club, on the theory that he sought revenge against Lingle for his refusal to help in reopening the club. Another theory soon surfaced about a St. Louis gang that might have had a reason to plot the murder of Lingle. Throughout the summer the police arrested and then released gang members.

Al Capone, who suffered most from the post-St. Valentine's Day police crackdown, decided that somebody had to pay for the Lingle killing. Moran, Kaufman, Ted Newberry and the pimp, Jack Zuta, were Capone's first targets. Zuta was the first to go when he was gunned down on August 1, 1930, in a summer resort near Delafield, Wisconsin. Newberry was killed a little while later. Kaufman fled to New York, where he eventually started a new career running a wire service and also began a successful career in gambling and prostitution. He became one of the bridges to the movement to the West led by men like "Bugsy" Siegel and Meier Lansky. Moran survived but was left powerless in Chicago, operating as a small-time thief until his death from natural causes.

Finally, as one source theorized, Capone, who never liked to turn a gang member over to the police, but preferred to do his own executions, turned over the "man who killed Lingle," Leo Vincent Brothers, originally from St. Louis. He was sentenced to 14 years, and was paroled eight years later. The sentence was light because the jury believed Brothers was "taking the fall" for someone else.

But what of Frankie, who by now had reportedly gone to New York and would soon be off to Nevada and new adventures in gambling after the end of Prohibition in 1932. His recorded encounters with the law were infrequent after the Lingle affair. On April 13, 1932, the *Chicago Tribune* announced in banner headlines: "Frankie Foster Guilty of Vagrancy in California." The next day, the *Tribune* headlined: "Frankie Foster Gets Six Months and a Fine of $500."

On April 24, 1938, the *New York Times* reported that Frankie Foster had been arrested by Federal agents in Reno, Nevada for an alleged holdup with an accomplice in New York City. After a four-day hearing, the Nevada judge released Frankie, refusing, on testimony of witnesses, to extradite him. The judge believed the witnesses who testified that Frankie and his wife Dorothy had not left Reno "since arriving in Nevada in 1935." It appears to have been the last time that Frankie's name appeared in newspapers in connection with a crime. His family believes he spent the rest of his life working at casinos in Nevada and California. In any event, he disappeared from public view, while maintaining contact with some members of his family. He died on April 23, 1967, in North Hollywood, California.

Frankie's early life was fairly typical of the poor East European Jewish immigrants who flocked to America in the late 19th and early 20th centuries. Most of them lived on Chicago's West Side and worked in various trades. Frankie's family came to America from Romania, where their name was Frost; other members of his family went to England. Frankie was the eldest of eight children—two boys and six girls. Frankie, a good looking lad, went to public school on the West Side. His father died when Frankie was 19, and it fell on him to support the family. He quit school and went to work as a bookkeeper for a neighborhood food merchant. Because the money he earned there was apparently insufficient to support the large family, he joined the "business" of Dion O'Banion, who had already seen the potential for profit in the new Prohibition laws.

Frankie met "Nails" Morton another Jewish "thug" who made a great deal of money working with O'Banion, the Irish gangster from Maxwell Street who appears to have worked with a number of Jewish associates. By 1930, O'Banion, Morton and Weiss were all dead and George "Bugs" Moran was the leader of the North Side gang; Frankie appears to have been one of his "boys." After Lingle's murder, Frankie first went to New York and then to the West, thus escaping the rest of the murderous wars that Capone was waging in Chicago until he was arrested by the "Untouchables" and convicted of income tax evasion.

As Ira Eisenberg recalls in his article, and several of Frankie's nephews and nieces confirm, Frankie supported his family during their time of need and "on Friday nights would bring some of his cronies for dinner, and leave behind the money his mother and three youngest sisters required for the coming week."

Research indicates that Frankie Foster made his living illegally, as did many other young immigrants, but not as a "hit man" for Al Capone, "Bugs" Moran or others. While Chicago Jews were members of gangs in Chicago, and much has been written on this, they were not known to be "killers for hire," at least not in Chicago. But the most important fact, of course, is that Frankie was released after a hearing because there was insufficient evidence to hold him for the murder of Jake Lingle. While he got into trouble with the police several times, he was always released and never convicted of a crime. American law holds that a man is presumed innocent until he is proven guilty. The headline that so alarmed Mr. Eisenberg's mother should have been supplanted by another headline: "Frankie Foster Found Innocent of the Jake Lingle Murder."

Part II

Business in the City

6

Albert Davis Lasker: "The Father of Modern Advertising"

This is a biography of an extraordinary person who was born in Germany as an American citizen, came to Chicago at the age of eighteen and lived here for over forty years. During that time, he developed new advertising methods that helped him amass a great fortune, win a place in Chicago's elite Jewish society and become a great benefactor to both profitable and charitable enterprises. His name was Albert Davis Lasker.

Albert was born on May 1, 1880, in Freiberg, Germany, when his parents, American citizens, were visiting their German homeland. His father, Morris, born in 1840, was an American immigrant of liberal views who had settled in Galveston, Texas, where Albert lived until he left for Chicago when he was 18 years old.

Morris and the Lasker family originally came from a town named Lask, in what was Germany/East Prussia, but which is now in Poland. The Laskers were peddlers in Europe. Morris received a good education in early life and looked forward to a classic education. But in 1856, when Morris was 16 years old, he decided to emigrate to the United States, as did thousands of Germans in the aftermath of the social uprisings in 1848. Anti-Semitism grew, making it difficult for liberal-minded, educated Jews like Morris to pursue an intellectual life. Morris landed in Virginia, but decided to move on to Texas, which was open to immigrants and offered employment opportunities, if not intellectual ones.

When the Civil War began, Morris, who believed in the Union, found himself living in a small town in Texas which joined the Confederacy. Morris later wrote that he had no choice but to fight with the South, despite his Union sympathies. After the Civil War, Morris and a partner became traveling peddlers, riding a mule wagon on desolate Texas trails selling merchandise of all types. Soon he found himself in Galveston, where he set up the Lasker Real Estate Company. He also opened a number of banks, which became very successful.

Morris had an older brother, Eduard who remained in Germany after Morris left and became one of the best-known Jewish lawyers, publicists and liberal politicians in Germany. He was one of the first Jews strong enough to openly attack anti-Semitism. Eduard supported Otto Bismarck in his campaign to unite the German states, and he is often cited as one of the architects of the plan of unification. After the Franco-Prussian War in 1870, Bismarck (often known as the "Iron Chancellor") succeeded in forming a united Germany, but he turned against the Liberal Party of which Eduard was a leader, and it became Bismarck's ambition "to break the hated Jew." He did so after a bitter struggle, and in 1879 Eduard lost his seat in the Reichstag. In 1883 Eduard, a much admired figure in the Lasker family, came to visit with Morris and his family in Galveston, but died unexpectedly a year later in New York of a heart attack. The United States Congress passed a resolution memorializing Eduard for his devotion to "free liberal ideas."

Morris had married a young woman who was a third generation German Jewish American. Her name was Nettie Heidenheimer Davis (the last name replacing her father's German name of "Schmulian"). Morris and Nettie had eight children, who went to public school in Galveston and apparently led happy lives. Some were later involved in Jewish and Zionist organizations. Morris's banks and a new milling business were prospering and Morris soon became an important person in Galveston society even though he was Jewish.

Then in 1893 a great financial panic gripped the United States. Morris's banks and real estate business collapsed suddenly. Morris sent his family to Germany for a year because life there was cheaper. Albert, however, stayed with his father in Texas. They closed their large house and Morris and his son lived in a small rented room. As time passed, Morris was able to rebuild his business, enabling him to resume his path to richness. He became a shrewd grain trader and was elected President of the Galveston Cotton Exchange. Later, he ran for state senator in Texas and served for one term.

Albert went through his early schooling like a "flash." A highly precocious boy, he decided to go into business on his own at the age of twelve. He wrote, edited and published a four-page newspaper called the *Galveston Free Press*, for which he also sold advertising. The paper, copies of which are still available in archives, was an immediate success.

He wrote of local problems and matters dealing with the theater in which he was interested: "Sarah Bernhardt returned to France;" he reported, and "The divorce case of Leslie Carter and his wife to have rehearing in the Superior Court of Illinois." He also published some jokes: "With what were you particularly struck, when you went on the stage?" "[with] Two bricks."

In high school Albert was in charge of a good many things, including the school magazine. At the age of thirteen he was the "Big Man" in the school, and also became manager of the football team.

Albert never forgot the Panic of 1893 (just as a later generation would not forget the Great Depression of 1929). He commented to a friend 30 years later that he would never invest in real estate again after what had happened in 1893.

Albert, while in high school, also worked in Morris's business, learning all the tricks of the trade. In 1896, he graduated from high school, decided not to go on to college, and joined the staff of the *Galveston News* at a salary of $40 per week, a goodly amount for the time.

Albert's career as a journalist ended, however, rather suddenly in 1898. He apparently wrote a review for his newspaper of a play that he had never seen because he went out of town on the night the play was to be performed. The next morning his review appeared, but the theater had burned down the evening before the play was to be performed. Albert was humiliated. (A brief escapade with a young lady seems to have taken him out of town.) He quit the newspaper, and father and son decided that Albert should leave Galveston temporarily; Morris deciding that journalism was the wrong career for his brilliant son.

Morris was owed a favor by Lord & Thomas, an advertising agency in Chicago. Representatives of that agency came to Galveston and offered Albert, who was then 18, a position with their Chicago firm. Albert accepted with reluctance, since it meant leaving his father. Despite his close relationship with Morris, Albert rarely visited Texas after his move to Chicago because of his journalistic debacle in Galveston. Albert was to stay with Lord & Thomas in Chicago for over 40 years, until 1942.

Morris died in 1916 at 76. He was a venerated figure in Galveston and left a substantial fortune, mostly in real estate. Albert, as the Executor of his father's estate, sold all of Morris's real estate holdings. Later a huge oil field was discovered on this land, and it is said that Albert could have died a billionaire rather than a mere multimillionaire if he had kept his father's land. Albert's mother, Nettie, died in 1936 in New York City.

Albert came to Chicago in 1898 to work as a clerk at Lord & Thomas in an office then located near Marshall Field's Department Store on State Street (now Macy's). His salary was $10.00 a week for his first year on the job. After that, he began to solicit accounts in person, on foot and by rail, then an unheard-of method of selling advertising as a "product." His salesmanship was an immediate success. Albert asked Lord & Thomas to give him accounts that were losing money, and he was successful with these as well. Within a very short time, his aggressive salesmanship and excellent advertising copy so impressed Lord & Thomas, that in 1903 when Lord retired, Albert was able to purchase his share and become a partner at the age of 24.

At this time, he met one John E. Kennedy, reportedly a famous Canadian "Mountie" who wrote advertising for the Hudson Bay Company and for patent medicines like Dr. Shoop's Restorative. Albert was impressed by Kennedy and his advertising style, recalling that Kennedy told him "that advertising is simple." "He told me 'Advertising is salesmanship in print.'"

The typical advertising of the day repeated the product's name with a catchphrase. Lasker dismissed this kind of advertising as "sloganizing." Kennedy taught him that in an ad, the unique benefit of the product should be identified and promoted (even though, in truth, the benefit might not be unique or even of actual benefit). An illustration in an ad should not be "art for art's sake," but should add emphasis to the message of the copy, just as an editorial cartoon adds punch to the text of the editorial.

Kennedy was hired by Lord & Thomas and America's first advertising copywriting training program was born. The firm grew tremedously, hiring many reporters and teaching them to write successful copy. In 1907 when Kennedy left to run his own business, Albert hired Claude Hopkins, already a successful advertising writer, to replace him. Hopkins worked for the company for the next 18 years.

Albert began to introduce new products for new clients with enormous success. During his career, Albert worked for nearly 400 accounts. Four of these in particular were Palmolive, Pepsodent, Kotex and Lucky Strike.

He took a soap developed by a small firm from palm and olive oils, and called it Palmolive, the "best selling soap in the World." His slogan for Palmolive, "Keep that schoolgirl complexion," made it a worldwide best seller.

His slogan introducing Pepsodent toothpaste—"No Dingy Film—See How Teeth Shine Without It"—was a success, made even greater when Albert hired Bob Hope to represent Pepsodent on the radio.

Albert created a merchandising as well as an advertising breakthrough for Kotex. Women had always had to ask the pharmacist for sanitary napkins, which caused embarrassment. Albert commissioned the design of a Kotex box that could be displayed openly on store shelves, and created advertising—"How the Society Woman, the Debutante, Meets the Demands of Daily Modern Life." The advertising of sanitary napkins had been taboo until Albert's firm made Kotex one of the Kimberly-Clark's best-selling products. Albert became a major Kimberly-Clark shareholder.

For Lucky Strike cigarettes, Albert used the phrase "Reach for a Lucky Instead of a Sweet," an all-too successful appeal to women who represented a previously untapped market. The American Tobacco Company, which owned Lucky Strike, became a huge client for Lord & Thomas. Albert fought attempts by doctors and cancer prevention groups to print a warning about the dangers of smoking on cigarette packages. He felt it was an invasion of freedom of speech and that Americans should decide for themselves whether to smoke or not.

Albert's extraordinary energy and business acumen brought him many successes outside the advertising world. The fortune he amassed in the years prior to 1942, of course, helped him to gain considerable status in the community.

He was particularly interested in politics. Like his father, he was a Republican, as were many Jews after the Civil War—it was the party of Abraham Lincoln, the great hero of the Union cause. Like his father, he was an isolationist, believing that European wars and religious strife should be avoided by America at all costs. Albert was a follower of Theodore Roosevelt, whom he knew and liked. After the end of World War I, Albert joined Teddy Roosevelt's campaign against President Woodrow Wilson and his support for the League of Nations.

Then in 1919, Roosevelt died and Wilson suffered an incapacitating stroke. The 1920 Presidential campaign thus became a wide open affair. Albert was a member of the Republican National Committee, contributing a great deal of money and his advertising skills to the campaign. He had huge posters created boosting the Republican presidential candidate Warren Harding, calling Harding an "Old Fashioned Sage" who could be relied on to return the nation to post-war "normalcy." Among the Democrats opposing Harding was a rising young politician, Franklin D. Roosevelt, who wanted America to join the League of Nations. The rest is history—After Harding was elected President in 1920, Albert resigned from the Republican National Committee and returned to work full time at Lord & Thomas.

In the meantime, he had become deeply involved with his beloved baseball. In 1916, he had bought a majority interest in the Chicago Cubs; his friend William Wrigley purchased a minority interest. Then in 1919 came the notorious White Sox scandal involving the bribery of baseball players. Albert almost single-handedly brought about the creation of a commission of Club owners to deal with the scandal. He worked with a Chicago attorney, Alfred S. Austrian and his partners at a prominent Chicago Jewish law firm, to have a Federal judge, Kenesaw Mountain Landis, appointed as the first Commissioner of Baseball with authority to deal with the so-called "Black Sox" scandal and future problems as they arose. For reasons not readily apparent—perhaps he disliked owning a "loser"—Albert sold his interest in the Chicago Cubs to Wrigley in 1925. Wrigley's family eventually sold the team to the Chicago Tribune Company. Albert and Wrigley maintained a business connection; when the Wrigley Building was completed in 1924, Lord & Thomas was among the first businesses to move into the prestigious new skyscraper, the first major building north of the Chicago River on Michigan Avenue.

Albert's interest in sports then switched mainly to golf, which he played with the pros at his 18-hole golf course on his magnificent Mill Road estate in Lake Forest, for which he spent more than $4,000,000. The estate was noted for its beautiful gardens, pools, hiking trails and wooded areas. In its center was a 50-room French-style manor house. In 1939 he donated the entire estate to the University of Chicago as a research and recreation facility.

Albert was appointed by President Harding to head the U.S. Shipping Board, a very important position in the Government in the early 1920s. In Washington, he undertook the difficult job of settling a huge shipping scandal that had engulfed the Board, and supervised the building of a new fleet of ships—his great organizational skills earned him much good will. But by 1922, he had again returned to Chicago and his firm where his fortune grew immensely. In addition to his Lake Forest estate, he built a beautiful house in Glencoe adjoining the Lake Shore Country Club. Later the family also lived in an 18-room mansion at Burton Place and Dearborn Parkway on Chicago's near North side.

As Albert's wealth grew, he became friends with Chicago's Jewish elite. Among them was Louis Eckstein, the original donor of the land on which the Ravinia Music Pavilion stands. Albert's closest friend was said to be John Hertz, the founder of the Yellow Cab Company, and Albert's partner in business ventures. Albert always credited John Hertz with selling most of the securities held in their joint account just before November 1929. Hertz himself owned a beautiful farm in Cary, near Lake Forest, where he raised racehorses, including a winner of the Kentucky Derby.

As the Depression deepened, Albert helped many of his friends financially. He was close to the Harold Foreman family, which owned a majority interest in one of Chicago's largest banks; his daughter was married to one of the Foreman sons. Although he advanced $2,000,000 to the Bank, Albert could not save it from being absorbed by the First National Bank of Chicago. While he lost his $2,000,000 investment, he did serve as a director of the First National Bank for many years.

Albert began to question some of the policies of the Republican Party, particularly those of President Hoover through the early 1930's. Later, with the rise of anti-Semitism in Nazi Germany, Albert began to modify his isolationism. He respected many of the policies of Franklin D. Roosevelt and met with him at the White House. He backed the Lend-Lease program to assist a beleaguered England, which many Republicans opposed. He broke with the isolationist wing of the Republican Party and his good friend Robert Maynard Hutchins, Chancellor of the University of Chicago, who remained a staunch isolationist until the Japanese attacked Pearl Harbor.

In the 1940 Presidential campaign, Albert again became active in politics as a floor leader of the Illinois Delegation to the Republican convention, and in heading the campaign of Wendell L. Wilkie, a liberal Republican candidate nominated to oppose Franklin D. Roosevelt. Wilkie of course lost to Roosevelt, but he did introduce a more internationalist outlook into the Party.

Whatever the reason, and many are offered by different writers, in 1942 Albert decided to retire from Lord & Thomas and leave Chicago. Whether it was the War or just plain boredom, he resigned as Trustee of the University of Chicago, a position he had held for over five years, liquidated his interest in Lord & Thomas and took over the cash and other assets of the business.

He transferred the customers and operating business to three of the principal officers of Lord & Thomas—Emerson Foote in New York, Fairfax Cone in Chicago, and Don Belding in Los Angeles, none of whom were Jewish. Albert solicited all his clients to continue with the new firm of Foote, Cone & Belding, and all but one chose to stay.

As was customary within the Chicago German Jewish elite, Albert was active in Jewish affairs, particularly in civil rights work and philanthropy. He was a director of the Jewish Charities of Chicago and a member of the executive board of the American Jewish Committee. The latter organization was active in the Leo Frank case involving the unjust arrest in 1914 of a young Jewish businessman in Atlanta for the alleged murder of a Gentile girl employed at his factory. Albert, with great courage, devoted almost a year of his time and contributed over $100,000 to defend Leo Frank, who was, despite all efforts, found guilty and then lynched by a mob.

Soon thereafter, Albert contributed $75,000 to the purchase of a farm in Pennsylvania where poor Russian Jewish immigrants could be taken from the city slums to be trained in agriculture. He also contributed money to Hadassah and other Jewish and Israeli organizations.

He was married three times. In 1902 he married Flora Warner, who was Jewish. Though severely ill in the early years of their marriage, she bore him three children and died in 1936 of cancer. They had two daughters, Mary (Mrs. Leigh B. Block, after her divorce from Gerhard Foreman), Frances (Mrs. Sidney Brody), and a son, Edward Lasker. Albert's daughter Mary and her husband Leigh Block were distinguished art collectors. In 1980 they donated funds to Northwestern University for the establishment of an art gallery in Evanston. The initial collection, which has grown through donations and purchases to approximately 4,000 works of art, is now housed at Northwestern's new Mary and Leigh Block Museum of Art, 40 Arts Circle Drive, where a wide range of the University's fine arts activities take place.

His second marriage, to Doris Kenyon Sills Hopkins, a young screen actress, ended in divorce in 1939 after about a month.

His third marriage, in 1940, was to Mary Woodward Reinhardt, who was at his side when he passed away. She was a loving wife and a superb gardener, and she initiated and supervised much of Albert's philanthropic projects. Among them were large donations for Cancer Research to the Lasker Foundation at the University of Chicago, and for financial study and research in the field of degenerative disease and birth control.

In 1942 Albert and Mary created the Lasker Foundation, which to this day grants prestigious awards to researchers and scientists.

In 1950, two years before his death, Albert and his wife visited Israel. He called this trip the "high point of his life." For the first time, he declared, "he understood the concept of the Jewish people."

In spite of his successes in business, public service and philanthropy, Albert appeared to have often felt like an outsider of American society, and spent a great deal of his life as a "loner." In Glencoe the Jewish elite built their own country club since they were refused membership in the Gentile clubs. In the advertising business in which Jews were a minority, Albert operated his firm without any partners. Perhaps that is why Israel had such an appeal to him, at least in the short run.

Albert Davis Lasker died on May 30, 1952. Private funeral services were held at the Lasker residence at 29 Beckman Road, in New York City. His wife Mary died in 1994.

7

Ernest Byfield: The Pump Room and the Pageant

Recently I had the pleasure of dining at the Pump Room in the Ambassador East Hotel, 1301 North State Parkway. Across from the Pump Room is a sitting area called the "Ernest Byfield Room." My visit reminded me of research material I had gathered some years ago from Byfield's family and from the many newspaper articles, books and magazine articles that had been written about Ernest Byfield. The contributions of Ernest Byfield and his father to Chicago in the entertainment and hotel fields are worth remembering.

In his book *Sabers and Suites: The Story of Chicago's Ambassador East* (1983), Rick Kogan writes: "Ernest Byfield was born in Chicago shortly after midnight on November 3, 1889. He died at 6:20 a.m. on February 10, 1950. It was Friday. A heart attack." Chicago newspapers splashed the news of Byfield's death on their front pages, and published long and generous articles praising his spectacular accomplishments. A graveside funeral service was held at Rosehill Cemetery. Humphrey Bogart and Lauren Bacall, who celebrated their wedding at the Pump Room, were at the funeral, as was then Chicago Mayor Martin Kennelly. There was no rabbi reading Jewish prayers; friends and family members gave the eulogies.

Ernest ("Ernie") Byfield was descended from ancestors who were innkeepers in a small town near Budapest, Hungary. His father, Joseph, came to Chicago in 1867 when he was 14 years old. (He anglicized the family name of "Beifeld" to Byfield.) Joseph got a job in a dry-goods store on State Street run by Marshall Field and Levi Z. Leiter. Joseph was said to be a "human calculator" in bookkeeping and soon became an important figure in the business, which ultimately became "Marshall Field & Company" (now Macy's). During the Great Chicago Fire of 1871, Joseph made a deep impression on Field and Leiter by helping them move their goods out of the path of the fire, which destroyed their store.

Joseph and his brother then decided to go into business on their own. Through the help of a speculator, they took on some of the operation of the White City amusement park at 62nd Street and South Parkway (now Martin Luther King, Jr. Drive). It was fashioned after the successful Midway at the World's Columbian Exposition of 1893, with a huge Ferris wheel.

Joseph was very interested in getting back into the family business of innkeeping, and purchased the Sherman House at Clark and Randolph in 1902 for $200,000. It was a bargain for Joseph, a location in the heart of Chicago's downtown and a great historic site. Abraham Lincoln had stayed in the first Sherman structure in 1847. The second Sherman Hotel was built in 1861, rebuilt in 1871 after the Great Fire, and rebuilt by Joseph in 1911. It featured a restaurant called "The Battery" which enjoyed a fine reputation.

The Sherman House was demolished in 1980 to be replaced by the James R. Thompson Center, a mixed-use government and commercial building, promoted by, and named for, a living former Governor of Illinois. A plaque in the lobby reads "This marks the site in Illinois on which a hotel has been continuously maintained." The architecturally bold new building is sometimes referred to as "Hotel Thompson."

Ernie is quoted as saying he was first offered a job to work at the Sherman when he was 17 years old, after attending school at the

Armour Institute and Cornell College. Like his father, Ernie was a mathematical wizard, but he soon tired of devoting all his time to keeping track of the hotel's complicated bookkeeping details. In due course he set out to widen his horizons and "learn the 1000 things that a hotelman should know."

Joseph Byfield died in September, 1926. Ernie, together with his confidant, Frank West Bering, assumed management of the Sherman. They also took control of the Ambassador, an old residential hotel located in the Gold Coast at the corner of State Parkway and Goethe Street, another historic, elegant area. Byfield and his partner also became interested in a piece of vacant property to the east of the Ambassador, and they soon took steps to acquire this lot and to construct the Ambassador East Hotel. The two hotels became prestigious places of residence as well as stopover sites for famous travelers. There was also a large restaurant, later to be called the Pump Room. As a novel feature, the two Ambassador hotels were connected by an underground tunnel, housing tobacco and barber shops and other amenities.

Ernest also turned his attention to a club operating at the Sherman, called the College Inn. The name had come from Ernie's and his father's belief that the "nightclub was inextricably tied up with Heidelberg collegians drinking beer . . ." It was here that Ernie began to host celebrities. He made it a gathering place for stars, like George M. Cohan, Ethel Barrymore, Billie Burke, the Dolly sisters and "hundreds of others." Ernest employed jazz musicians instead of the customary string ensemble. He conceived new shows for his club, like an ice show. He turned the College Inn into a Panther Club, with a jungle décor and waiters in "leopard skin" jackets serving tropical drinks. He hired Gene Krupa and his band and other famous bands. But, the Club apparently was not profitable.

The Great Depression severely affected the hotel industry, and the Sherman group, which included the Ambassador hotels, went through a bankruptcy proceeding in the 1930s, from which Ernie soon emerged still owning the three hotels.

In October, 1938, after recovering from his money troubles, Ernie opened the Pump Room to great aplomb and publicity. The restaurant was named after a well-known facility in Bath, England, where fashionable people gathered in the eighteenth and early nineteenth centuries to "take the waters."

The "waters" at Chicago's Pump Room were more likely to be alcoholic. Rick Kogan writes: "At his Pump Room, the celebrities got the best tables. The Social Register and Blue Book people, with a few notable and wealthy exceptions, took what was left. And through the power of Byfield's personality and his uncanny sense of self-promotion, stars soon became more concerned with their Byfield rating than their fan mail." The most desired booth was located to the right of the entrance. The famous actress Gertrude Lawrence, then in a starring role at the Harris Theater, was said to have been the first celebrity to have dined in Booth One.

Hundreds of framed photographs of the stars that visited the Pump Room still hang on the walls outside the Room—unfortunately without names to identify them. The meals and services at the Pump Room are still legendary. Flaming sword dishes were most spectacular. As Jack Benny was reported to have said: "They'll serve anything on a flaming sword except the check."

The Pump Room reached the height of its fame in the 1940s. Ronald Reagan, Clark Gable, Richard Burton, Elizabeth Taylor, and William Holden were there. Irv Kupcinet began writing his column for the *Chicago Sun-Times* in 1943, and he and his wife Essie often dined at the Pump Room to pick up celebrity news. "Kup" later built a replica of Booth One in his apartment.

Friends of Ernie have been quoted as saying that his public energy and humor masked "considerable frustrations and insecurities." His first wife was Gladys Rosenthal, a Chicago socialite and golf champion. Her wealthy father, Benjamin J. Rosenthal, was the founder of the Chicago Mail Order Company, later known as Aldens. Two sons were born of this marriage, Hugh and Ernest, Jr. Gladys was the Illinois golf champion, a considerable feat for a woman, and a Jewish one to boot. Ernie often referred to himself as "The Squaw Man of Golf." Gladys and Ernie were divorced in 1928.

Ernie remarried, to a beautiful socialite, Kathryn (Kitty) Priest Rand, who soon divorced him, after Ernie told the media that they had an "ideal marriage." One child, a daughter, Jean, was born of this marriage. Ernie's third wife, who survived him, was Adele Sharpe Thomas, a beauty salon owner 30 years his junior. His estate was estimated at $300,000. He left one-third of his estate to his wife and the balance in trust for his three children.

With respect to his life as a Jew, little is now remembered. Only his first wife was Jewish. However, research has revealed an interesting article published in the Sentinel on February 23, 1950 under the headline, "Friend Writes Epitaph to Late Ernie Byfield." It was written by Leo Ellis a manager of the Sherman Hotel:

> We have lost a great friend, Mr. Ernest Byfield.
>
> I do not believe that many people knew the part he played in helping the cause of many charitable organizations. During the war years, Mr. Byfield was always ready to extend his services for any good cause. Many a time Mr. Byfield, as Chairman, and I, as Co-Chairman, have filled the Chicago Stadium with thousands of people, the proceeds of these affairs going to many Jewish charities. I was closely associated with him in all these undertakings, and know there was no man who gave of his efforts more freely in spite of the heavy schedules of his regular business.
>
> During the war years we both worked on Bond drives, for the Red Cross, Servicemen's centers, and many other efforts for which we received citations from the Navy, Civilian Defense, the Red Cross and others.
>
> In 1943, when Ben Hecht, Billy Rose, Moss Hart and Kurt Weil approached Mr. Byfield to help with the Palestinian problems, he unhesitatingly plunged into the organization of a gigantic Pageant ["We Will Never Die"] which was staged in the Chicago Stadium.

> He was elected as Chairman of this Pageant and this writer as Co-Chairman. He did a Herculean job, but was satisfied when he saw the climax of all his work at the Chicago Stadium where over 20,000 people had gathered.
>
> As late as October of 1949, when I approached him to help the Denver Sanatorium for tubercular patients in holding a dinner in our Hotel Sherman, he immediately telephoned George Jessel and persuaded him to be Master of Ceremonies at this affair.
>
> His good-heartedness and complete devotion to charitable causes made him one of the greatest men I have ever known.

The October 23, 1966, *Chicago Tribune* Sunday Magazine section carried a feature article headlined: "Why are They Doing This to Ernie Byfield?" It recounted Ernie's life and his accomplishments as the "perfect hotelman." The article notes that "All trains met Ernie Byfield . . . the distinguished guests who stopped off in Chicago made the Pump Room their first port of call."

The *Tribune* article describes the ceremony held at the Pump Room to honor Ernie's memory, where a bust of Byfield dressed as Beau Nash was dedicated. [Richard "Beau" Nash (1674–1762), was Master of Ceremonies at Bath, which he turned from a sleepy health spa into the favorite resort of Britain's elite. He was a self-invented character, a celebrated dandy and leader of fashion.] The article concludes: "Byfield is gone from the scene, but the glittering Pump Room goes on . . . George Jessel, when he learned that his lifelong friend had died of a heart attack [remarked], "It couldn't have been a heart attack . . . Ernie Byfield gave his heart to his friends many years ago."

Ben Hecht was a good friend of Byfield and often visited the Pump Room. Undoubtedly, it was Ben Hecht, then deeply involved with the Bergson Group, and had written the script for the Pageant "We Will Never Die" who convinced Byfield to be the Chairman of the Pageant and to engage in other Zionist activities of the Group during World War II.

8

William S. Paley: Good Night, and Good Luck

In the recent film "Good Night and Good Luck," a docu-drama about the Ed Murrow television show, the enigmatic figure of William S. Paley (played by actor Frank Langella) is often seen in the background, supervising the program's battle with Senator Joseph McCarthy and his campaign to "expose" and blacklist those it designated as subversives or worse. In reviewing the film, Roger Ebert of the *Chicago Sun Times* characterized Paley "as the boss who ran the network as a fiefdom, but granted Murrow independence from advertiser pressure."

Paley, beginning as a young man in his late twenties, had built a huge radio empire by acquiring numerous small stations, and combining them under the name Columbia Broadcasting System, Inc. He had become President and principal owner of CBS and a leading pioneer in radio news.

He was born in Chicago on September 28, 1901, to Samuel Paley and his wife, Goldie Drell Paley. Both were born in Kiev, Ukraine, and immigrated to the United States with hundreds of thousands of Jews who fled Russia and its pogroms after the assassination of Czar Alexander II. About seventy-five thousand of these Russian immigrants settled in Chicago.

Samuel Paley, was born in 1875, came to Chicago with members of his family in 1883 and married Goldie Drell in 1896. The Paley family first lived on West 14th Street, about a block from the corner of Maxwell and Halsted Streets. Samuel's father Isaac was said to have been a handsome secular Jew, not religious and quite successful even under the onus of Russian anti-Semitism. William later wrote that he had probably inherited his enterprising business acumen from his grandfather.

By 1901, the Paley family had moved to 1767 Ogden Avenue, a somewhat better neighborhood a mile from Maxwell Street. Here Samuel Paley started a new business manufacturing and selling cigars. In the family living quarters behind the store William Paley was born. By 1905, the Paleys were able to move to 395 South Marshfield Avenue, near Jackson Boulevard—another step up the social ladder.

For reasons that are not clear, Samuel moved his family and his cigar business to Detroit when William was four years old, only to return to Chicago a few years later. In 1910, Samuel moved his company into a large factory building in Chicago at 235 West Van Buren Street. It was said that he had more than 75 employees. He started and became President of the Congress Cigar Company, located in a larger facility at 404 Racine. In 1917 the family moved to 1456 West Fargo Avenue, on the far North side. It was their last home address in Chicago.

It was said that "William lived for his father's approval." Though a strict disciplinarian, Samuel had deep affection for his son and taught him every detail of the tobacco business. William led a sheltered existence as a boy, growing up in an "extended family," descendants of whom still live in the Chicago area, attending good schools and having many friends, most of whom were Jewish. He was also greatly interested in the opposite sex.

After graduating from Schurz High School, William attended Western Military Academy at Alton, Illinois, an expensive private school and then he went to the University of Chicago for one year. When the family moved to Philadelphia in 1918, William transferred to the Wharton School of Finance at the University of Pennsylvania. According to Robert Motz, author of *CBS: Reflections on a Bloodshot Eye* (1975), William felt he was discriminated against when he applied to a fraternity (ZBT) at Wharton, not only by Gentiles but also by German Jews because his family came from Russia, But. he was accepted into Zeta Beta Tau, the most prestigious fraternity, and was elected president of his chapter.

After graduating from Wharton in 1922, he joined the Congress Cigar Company. His father had continued to teach William the cigar business, from manufacturing to finance, even sending him to tobacco farms in Cuba during the summers so he could learn about growing tobacco. By 1925, William had been promoted to advertising manager/president/secretary of the Congress Cigar Company and given an equity interest in the business. His salary was $30,000 a year, a considerable amount for that time.

Labor problems had caused Samuel Paley to move the business from Chicago to Philadelphia in 1918. There had been conflicts from the time of the Haymarket tragedy, complaints by workers who felt they were grossly underpaid by the manufacturers, many of whom were Jewish. Samuel Gompers, a Jewish leader of the American Federation of Labor (AFL), led the campaign against the owners. Samuel Paley and his fellow manufacturers decided to move their businesses to locations where union activity was not as strong or militant as Chicago. Samuel Paley, his brother Jacob and their families took with them to Phildelphia all the resources of the Congress Cigar Company including its popular La Palina brand cigar. Much has been written about the origin of the name and its logo. Was the name a tribute to Goldie Paley, and was it originally her portrait that was later transformed into a colorful Cuban beauty?

The brand was a colossal success: the Paley cigar business eventually had many large factories in various Eastern locations. Then in 1931, as the Great Depression was beginning, Samuel and

William Paley and their partners (who owned minority interests), sold the business for 30 million dollars.

William's interest in radio seems to have begun while he was doing advertising for the Congress Cigar Company. The story is told by Ira Berkow in *Maxwell Street: Survival in a Bazaar* (1977). One summer while William's father and his uncle Jacob were traveling in Europe, William "took it upon himself to invest fifty dollars a week to put Miss La Palina and a ten-piece orchestra on a local station." When Samuel and Jacob returned, they were furious at what they considered a waste of money. They insisted that William cancel the program, but requests for the show by listeners began to come in to the station. Sales of cigars jumped, and "Bill Paley grew more and more interested in radio."

In 1928 William purchased his first group of radio stations, and by September 26, 1928, had become President of CBS. He moved quickly to make CBS a strong rival of David Sarnoff's NBC. CBS grew and prospered in the Depression of the 1930s. Paley brought great talent to CBS. He hired Bing Crosby, discovered Kate Smith and lured Jack Benny away from NBC.

It has been said that Paley turned down an option for the musical *Fiddler on the Roof* because, he remarked, "I couldn't do it because it's the story of my own family."

When he moved to New York, Paley wanted to join American cafe society, not just Jewish society. He pursued and married Dorothy Hart Hearst, who was divorced from John Randolph Hearst, son of William Randolph Hearst. William later divorced Dorothy and in 1947 married Barbara "Babe" Cushing Mortimer, a beautiful socialite born in Boston, the daughter of Johns Hopkins brain surgeon Dr. Harvey Cushing. She had been a fashion editor at *Vogue* and was the mother of two children by her first husband, oil heir Stanley Grafton Mortimer, Jr., whom she divorced in 1946. She and Paley had two children, Kate and Bill Jr. Because of her marriage to Paley, she lost her access to many Social Register functions, but she remained a widely admired fashion icon. Nevertheless

Paley carried on a string of extra-marital affairs, which wore on her nerves and affected her health. She became a heavy smoker, and in 1974 she was diagnosed with lung cancer. She died on July 6, 1978, the day after her 63rd birthday.

During World War II, William took a leave of absence from CBS to help organize radio operations for the Office of War Information in Europe. He was promoted to colonel and received medals for his service from the Americans as well as from the French and Italians.

William returned to CBS in 1946, and became Chairman of the *See It Now* television series, which later became known as *You are There*, hosted by Edward R. Murrow. The airing of this show by CBS was a courageous act; CBS came under powerful pressures to cease criticizing the McCarthy investigations. William supported Murrow's efforts at critical times, but the movie and some facts raise questions about Paley's behind-the-scenes role.

Paley was a careful, conservative man, and when a leading advertiser threatened to sever its ties with CBS because of Murrow's show, Paley shifted Murrow to the profitable celebrity interview show, *Person to Person*. Murrow's show was later moved to a minor slot and he lost his leading role as a commentator on American policy. McCarthy's activities had ceased, and CBS was no longer embattled in politics.

As for William's Jewish activities, they appear to have been limited to the United Jewish Appeal and the Philadelphia Jewish Federation. In earlier years in Chicago, his family appears to have belonged to a Reform temple, but there is no evidence that William joined any temple.

William died on October 26, 1990. He left his magnificent art collection, valued at several hundreds of millions of dollars, to the William S. Paley Foundation, which in turn gave the collection to the New York Museum of Modern Art. The rest of his estate was left to numerous other charities, some individuals and to his children and grandchildren.

A memorial service for Paley was held on November 12 at Temple Emanuel-El, on Fifth Avenue and 65th Street, with Rabbi Ronald Sobel presiding. Over 2,000 people attended, including past presidents and officers of CBS, and politicians, among whom was former President Richard M. Nixon, a friend of William's. Janet Murrow, Edward Murrow's widow, was there. William was interred in the Memorial Cemetery of St. John's Church, Cold Spring Harbor, New York next to his wife Barbara.

Five friends or colleagues eulogized Paley as the man who had more impact on the delivery of news and entertainment than any other person. Henry Kissinger, a close friend, said that while Paley enjoyed the company of politicians and world leaders, he did not allow them to influence his work. "He would never allow anything to interfere with his love affair with CBS."

Kissinger's remarks may give us some insight into both Paley's success and perhaps his limitations. After his spectacular success in building CBS and a great fortune for himself, he showed no inclination to become involved in future political events. He had achieved a great deal—he had moved from the Maxwell Street ghetto to Fifth Avenue in Manhattan. He had supported Edward R. Murrow at a critical moment in broadcasting history, and continued to lead the way for present day media.

As for the company William created, CBS was eventually purchased by Westinghouse Electric Corporation in 1995 and then by Viacom in 2000.

9

Elizabeth Stein, Photographer

The recording of oral histories often leads one to discover unexpected treasures of Chicago's past. They are surprising and totally unanticipated. Our Society has for some time been looking forward to taping and transcribing the life story of Elizabeth Stein, a resident of Chicago's Gold Coast, who is a great-granddaughter of Marcus Spiegel, a Chicagoan who was one of the highest ranking Jewish officers to serve in the Civil War, and who was killed in battle.

Marcus Spiegel's family came from Abendheim, a small town near Worms, Germany. They immigrated to Chicago beginning in the 1840s. It was a very large family, and their descendants included the Greenebaums, Felsenthals, Josephs, Schaffners, Spiegels and Harts—leading members of Chicago's early German-Jewish community.

We met Ms. Stein in her apartment, and it was instantly clear to us that we were in a remarkable place. Her home is filled with unique and beautiful art objects, paintings, and above all—her photographs.

Elizabeth Stein, we learned, had been an art teacher for over forty years, and during that period she had also become a splendid photographer. Her pictures have been exhibited locally and in galleries around the country. While advanced in years, Ms. Stein is still actively engaged in camera art, photographing the wide variety of subjects that inspire her.

The most recent local exhibition of her work was held last summer (1998) at Art and Paper Boy at 1351 West Belmont. Featured in the show were her memorable color prints of the Ringling Bros. Barnum & Bailey Circus. In the August 12 issue of *New City*, reviewer Michael Weinstein wrote:

> Still an active photographer at age 92, Elizabeth Stein has been shooting in color for 60 years, producing powerful images in a variety of genres. This career retrospective focuses on her circa-1940 circus documentary, but also includes stunning architectural shots and her most recent seductive and absorbing mandalas. Time has honed Stein's vision; the mandalas—segmented yet seamless compositions of dense patterns of vegetables, flowers and iron grillwork—concentrate her native intensity, eliminating anything that might interfere with single-minded meditation. The mandalas mark a shift from Stein's familiar fascination with the beauty of destructive forces; she has learned to turn power inward to achieve heightened awareness, rather than delivering our senses to exuberant sublime abandon, as with her 1992 shot of fire fighters spraying cascades of water on a building engulfed in billowing smoke.

Curator Ted Frankel wrote in his notes to the show:

> Art at Paper Boy is proud to exhibit a sampling of work by such an incredible woman. Through the years Elizabeth's photographs have been able to transform the ordinary into the extraordinary and document the times with a non-judgmental lens.
>
> I believe that Elizabeth Stein's ability to focus on a moment in time combined with her love of life and the eye of an artist has placed her forever on the short list of great women photographers.

The history that Elizabeth Stein was most eager to share with us was not about Marcus Spiegel, nor about her artistic work. She really wanted to tell us the story of her father Ernest Stein and his three brothers who began a business in Chicago in the late 1880s and achieved great financial success by creating and selling the world-famous "Paris Garter."

Albert Stein (the oldest of the brothers) came to Chicago via New York when he was about 20 years of age. He began to work in a wholesale house. In 1887 he decided to start a business of his own, with his brother Ernest soon joining him. They rented a room on Market Street near where the Civic Opera House now stands. In this room they began to manufacture men's garters, which they sold throughout the city to mercantile establishments. They also began handcrafting garters for women and children.

But the real growth in their business came when they bought a patent for men's garters to which they gave the name that denotes sophistication and high fashion—"Paris." They improved the Paris design by replacing its clumsy metal holder with a comfortable fastener, and adopted the advertising slogan, "no metal can touch you."

Soon the business added other products—foundation garments for women; belts and suspenders for men.

In 1906 A. Stein and Company acquired real estate at 1143 West Congress, erecting the first unit of a five-story plant designed by Alfred S. Alschuler, a well-known Chicago Jewish architect. By the 1920s the company was reported to be the largest manufacturer of garters in the world. The company's products were sold worldwide and its advertising budget was immense for its time. The "Paris Garter" was a fashion "must" for the well-dressed man.

The company was said to have earned a profit in every year of its existence. It became a public company in 1929, shortly before the start of the Great Depression, and its stock was listed on the New York Stock Exchange. The company earned about a million dollars that year. Albert Stein and Ernest Stein had died a short time earlier and another brother, Samuel Stein had become President.

In 1931 the Stein family decided to sell the company to the Kayser-Roth Corporation, a large industrial firm. The *Chicago Tribune*, in announcing the sale, reported:

> Owners of more than 55% of the common stock of A. Stein and Co., Chicago manufacturer of men's belts, garters and suspenders as well as foundation garments for women, Thursday agreed to sell their holdings to Kayser-Roth Corporation for $16,135,000 in convertible notes.

Abraham Freiler, son-in-law of Ernest Stein, remained as Chairman. Other members of the family continued to be employed by the company. Needless to say, the sale was well-timed. Within a generation, garters would be relics, replaced by elasticized socks.

Elizabeth Stein's oral history—detailing her own remarkable life and accomplishments has been transcribed by the Chicago Jewish Historical Society. Ms. Stein wanted to make sure that the "Paris Garter" would not be forgotten. This piece is written to reassure her that it will be remembered.

10

Mail Order & Bungalows: Philanthropist Benjamin J. Rosenthal

Benjamin Jefferson Rosenthal was born in Chicago on November 5, 1867, of Prussian German ancestry. Upon graduation from high school in 1884, he went to work for Gage Wholesale Millinery where he remained for several years.

In 1889, Rosenthal in association with his brother, Samuel, rented a small loft at Wabash and Congress Streets in Chicago, hired five employees and started the Chicago Mail Order Millinery Company. Louis Eckstein and Louis M. Stumer subsequently joined the new enterprise. They published a small catalog of their products. Undoubtedly the success of Julius J. Rosenwald's Sears Roebuck catalog influenced Rosenthal and his company. Be that as it may, Rosenthal became one of the founders of the mail order business which was to revolutionize merchandising in America for years to come, much as shopping through the Internet is doing today.

The first Chicago Mail Order Millinery Company catalog mailed by Rosenthal's company was the size of a pocket notebook. It displayed the unbelievably large hats of the day, packed with colorful flowers, veiling and feathers with prices ranging from $1.69 to $8.00.

In 1902, the company was incorporated in Illinois and its name was subsequently changed to Chicago Mail Order Company (called CMO for short).

As the number of women in the work force grew and bicycling became a national fad, women's fashions changed from bustles and long trailing skirts. CMO's business boomed as women ordered simpler attire through the catalog.

In 1905 the CMO catalog was expanded to 66 pages; in 1906 to 118 pages. As the business grew, the company moved to larger quarters at 14th and Wabash Streets. New merchandise lines continued to be added to the catalog. Handbags sold at prices ranging from 3 cents to $1.98, and a 70-inch beaver scarf sold for $6.48 (no tax). An 85-inch mink throw considered rather common in 1906, was listed at $4.98 in the catalog.

In 1909, CMO brought out its "big" catalog: 961 pages of fashions, toiletries, stoves, sewing machines, dining tables, bookcases, writing desks—and even a "monstrous" folding bed that could be disguised as a mantel during the day. As business flourished, CMO moved again, to a four-story building at 20th and Indiana Avenues. Employees' weekly wages ranged from $5 to $7, supplemented by a profit-sharing plan. Apparently a 25¢ corset cover was a "runaway" sales leader during this period. CMO continued to grow, despite an occasional economic depression.

A New York office was opened, but catalog merchandise was cut back to women's apparel and accessories, its original strength. Rosenthal retained substantial equity in the Company, but turned over management to others. As women's styles changed the catalog followed the trends. In 1928, CMO moved, yet again, to a large new building at 511 S. Paulina Street where it remained until recently. Its sales for 1929 were $26,400,000, a substantial amount for the times, but dropped to $19,000,000 in 1932.

By 1935 sales had dropped to $18,000,000, but CMO's catalog business survived the Great Depression. Late in the 1930s, installment sales and credit accounts were introduced. With Rosenthal's death on May 14 1936, CMO became a public company listed on the New York Stock Exchange.

In 1946, the Chicago Mail Order Company changed its name to "Aldens, Inc." to eliminate confusion with other Chicago mail order companies. Since"Aldens" had long been used as a private brand name on much of CMO's upscale merchandise, the transition was smooth. That year the catalog contained 638 pages. Aldens had become one of the leading mail order catalog companies in America, along with Sears Roebuck, Spiegel and Montgomery Ward—all of them Chicago-based. But by the mid-1970's, all of the mail order giants were in decline, Aldens, Inc. was sold, and its name disappeared.

While the catalog order business was Rosenthal's chief claim to fame in the business world, he was active in other fields. Together with his partners, Louis M. Stumer and Louis Eckstein, he was involved in millinery, cloak, suit and dress establishments, restaurants and drug stores. Emporium World Millinery, one of their largest enterprises, was a great success with sales of women's hats. The partners were also active in owning and managing real estate properties, and for good measure had outstanding success as magazine publishers: the *Red Book* and the *Blue Book*.

The Rosenthal group built three buildings on State Street on properties owned by the Chicago Board of Education, which signed 99-year leases with them beginning in 1890. One of these structures was the North American Building (36-44 South State Street, at the Northwest corner of State and Monroe Streets), a 19-story fireproof office building containing 147,563 square feet of rentable space. It had numerous tenants and was, in its day, one of the finest locations that a wholesale business could want. Two other buildings were owned by Rosenthal and his two partners. One was the Emporium Building (26-28 South State Street) a seven-story building occupied for many years by the Miller-Wohl Company, selling at retail ladies' ready-to-wear garments. The remaining building was the Mercantile Building (10-14 South

State Street), a six story building leased by S.S. Kresge Co. for their own use.

Rosenthal was married to Hannah Stumer (sister of Louis Stumer, one of his partners) on January 1, 1891. Rabbi Aaron A. Messing officiated at the ceremony. They had two daughters, Gladys and Elaine. Elaine was a well-known national golf champion at an early age. In 1995 she was elected to the Illinois Golf Hall of Fame. She was married to S.L. Reinhardt and later divorced. Gladys married Ernest Byfield, who became well known in Chicago as an owner of the Sherman and Ambassador West and East Hotels. They were subsequently divorced. Both girls later remarried.

Rosenthal himself was a lifelong Democrat. He ran for U.S. Congressman at Large from Illinois in 1914 on a "liberal" program, but lost the election. In his files is a letter from President Woodrow Wilson's office endorsing his candidacy. In 1919 after the end of World War I, he wrote a book called *Reconstructing America—Sociologically and Economically*. The foreword of the book contained Rosenthal's resume:

BENJAMIN J. ROSENTHAL'S RECORD

Served as Chairman of Chicago Committee on Unemployed, by appointment of Mayor Thompson. Succeeded in finding positions for hundreds of so-called "down and out-ers" who were lodged in the Municipal Lodging House of Chicago.

Founded Employment Committee for Men Past 45 Years of Age. This organization taken over afterwards by the Employers Association of Chicago, and later by the U.S. Government.

Founded Employment Committee for Employment of Crippled People and also for the employment of Colored Women. These Committees also taken over by the Department of Labor of the United States.

Introduced Bonus System and Profit Sharing in his various enterprises, which are among the most successful in the West.

Served as Chairman of the Merchant Marine Committee of the National Business League of America.

Sent abroad as Special Foreign Commissioner by the National Business League of America to investigate foreign commerce. Reported to a conference of business organizations, held in the Gold Room of Congress Hotel in Chicago, under the auspices of the National Business League of America.

Resolutions adopted by this conference for the restoration of the American Merchant Marine.

Wrote "The Need of the Hour: An American Merchant Marine" (1915), a volume which gained wide circulation and paved the way for the passage of the Shipping Bill.

Traveled throughout the United States, addressing various Chambers of Commerce on the Shipping Bill, which became a law. W.G. McAdoo wrote: You did great work for the Shipping Bill. The President recognizes, as I do, the great value of the public service you have rendered."

Early recognized the value of the Play Spirit in Modern Industrial and Commercial Life. Appointed Chairman of Finance Committee of Olympian Games Committee, and sent as one of the commissioners abroad to visit the foreign countries to arouse interest in the Olympian Games.

Served as a member of the Chicago Board of Education, 1894–1897.

Introduced in the public schools of Chicago the articulate method of teaching deaf mute children to replace sign method.

Appointed as one of the three examiners to examine the policy of Chicago for the first civil service examination, the other two being W.R. Stirling, Vice President, Illinois Steel Co., and W.T. Baker, ex-President of the World's Fair—both since deceased.

Served as Chairman of the Finance Committee of National Peace Jubilee held in Chicago at close of Spanish American War.

Served as Director of Chicago Association of Commerce.

Served as Director at various times of banks and other quasi-public organizations and institutions in Chicago and middle West.

In campaign for the re-election of Woodrow Wilson served as Treasurer of the Western Business Men's League.

Served as Member of U.S. Assay Commission by appointment of President Wilson

We commend the above record to the careful consideration of our readers.

THE PUBLISHER

Obviously, by 1919 Rosenthal was spending a great deal of his time on "good causes," such as upgrading the merchant marine, profit-sharing for his employees and adequate housing for workers. With regard to the latter, Rosenthal funded the development of single-family bungalows in Chicago in 1919. The Rosenthal Project called "Garden Homes" was a 175 unit development started at 8818 South Wabash Avenue, and subsidized by Rosenthal. It was his idea to build homes for the working class at a price they could afford. Working through the Chicago Dwellings Association, which he had founded, Rosenthal hired architect Charles Frost to design 133 detached bungalows and 21 duplexes. Though of different exterior design to avoid monotony, all had five rooms and the same interior design. The bungalows were a great success and bungalow developments spread to many parts of the city.

In 1922, Rosenthal created the Benjamin J. Rosenthal Foundation, which he dedicated to the pursuit of cultural activities and the "well-being of all citizens." The Chicago Jewish Historical Society is a recipient of grants from the foundation in support of several of the Society's activities. Rosenthal was an original trustee of the foundation, as was Henry Horner, an attorney, judge and later in the 1930's the first Jewish governor of Illinois. Among the Trustees of the foundation today are descendants of Rosenthal.

Through his foundation, Rosenthal also made grants to many worthwhile causes. For years his foundation also made annual awards to citizens who had distinguished themselves in public service. His foundation has carried on his traditions of making gifts for the "well-being of all citizens." Their contributions went to many different charities, including the Jewish Charities of Chicago and the National Conference of Christians and Jews. One of the major projects of the foundation was the provision of funding for the establishment of a year-round camp for inner city youths in Southern Michigan known as "The Benjamin J. Rosenthal and Hannah S. Rosenthal Camp."

Rosenthal was a member, among other organizations, of The Standard Club. A paragraph on his early life is contained in Meites' "History of the Jews of Chicago." His wife is listed as a sponsor of "The Romance of A People" in the booklet for Jewish Day (July 3, 1933) at the World's Fair of 1933.

Rosenthal lived for many years at the Ambassador Hotel, and maintained a summer home in Homewood, Illinois He died on May 14, 1936 at the age of 68, and was interred at Rosehill Cemetery. He was survived by his wife, two daughters, two granddaughters and three grandsons. His grandsons all served overseas with the American Armed Forces in World War II. Benjamin Jefferson Rosenthal, an American patriot all his life, undoubtedly would have been proud of them. Hannah Rosenthal, born in 1870, continued to live at the Ambassador Hotel until her death in 1970 at the age of 100.

11

Demise of the Foreman-State Bank: Was It "Shylock in Reverse"?

Early editions of the *Chicago Tribune* on Tuesday, June 9, 1931, carried a banner headline, "Thousands Awed by $200,000,000 Moving in Loop" over the following report: "While thousands of spectators stared with awe or curiosity a treasure valued at about $200,000,000 was moved through the blocked off streets of the Loop last night in the consummation of the merger of the Foreman-State bank with the First National group."

The story continued with a graphic description of the hundreds of policemen and special guards (with guns at the ready) who were posted on the streets as a fleet of armored trucks and other vehicles moved along late in the day from the corner of Washington and LaSalle Streets (33 N. LaSalle Street), site of the 40- story newly built Foreman-State Building went south on LaSalle Street to Monroe and east on Monroe to Clark to the First National Bank. There, all of the money, equipment and other assets of the Foreman-State Bank were unloaded to become part of the assets of First National.

America was in the midst of its worst recession and sinking into the Great Depression. Many banks had failed. Others, in danger of collapse, were forced to move their assets to stronger institutions and go out of business. The movement of the assets was part of the American scene in the summer of 1931, and it also marked the end of the Foreman-State Bank and its affiliates.

The third largest bank in Chicago at the time, the Foreman-State Bank was the largest and one of the oldest Jewish banks in the city. It's demise dealt a cruel blow to its investors, many of them Jews. Rumors were rife at the time, and persist to this day, that the Foreman family lost their bank to the First National because they were Jewish and thus did not receive financial support from other Chicago banks. A brief recap of the events leading to the ending of the Foreman-State Bank may be helpful in deciding whether anti-Semitism did indeed play a role in those events.

The first Foreman Bank was established in 1862 by Gerhard Foreman (1823-97), who immigrated from Darmstadt, Germany. He first moved to Delphi, Indiana and then to Chicago in 1857. The previous year he had married Hannah Greenbaum, whose family had established a mortgage-based lending institution in Chicago. Gerhard's bank prospered but was burned to the ground in the Great Fire of 1871, though it soon resumed business in new quarters in the Loop. Gerhard retired in 1885, transferring his interests to his sons, who conducted the business as a family partnership until 1897. In that year, the bank was incorporated as the Foreman Brothers Banking Company.

One of Gerhard's sons, Oscar G. Foreman, became most prominent in the management of the business; first becoming Vice-President, and then President in 1915. In 1923, the bank, having grown substantially both in the Loop and in outlying areas, was reorganized as the Foreman National Bank and the Foreman Trust and Savings Bank, with Oscar as Chairman and Harold E. Foreman, a third generation Foreman, as President.

Then, in 1929, came a momentous step—in hindsight, ill-timed in view of economic events soon to come. The Foreman Bank merged with the State Bank of Chicago, which eventually made the merged institution one of the three largest banks in Chicago.

The State Bank of Chicago had been established in 1889 by Helge A. Haugran and John J. Lindgren.both of Norwegian descent. The State Bank's deposits had grown to over $64,000,000, and it had many branches in outlying areas of Chicago. All of the State Bank's assets were transferred to the Foreman Bank in December, 1929. Harold Foreman was made Chairman of the directorate, Walter Head, from Omaha, Nebraska, was made President, and Oscar Foreman became Chairman of the Executive Committee. Stocks of both companies were selling at about $1,200 a share when, in July 1929, the merger was agreed to.

In October 1929 came the great market crash that signaled the economic depression. Throughout 1930 and early 1931, as the Hoover administration was unable to halt the downward spiral, businesses began to fail, which in turn quickly endangered banks, particularly the smaller ones whose borrowers defaulted on their loans.

In "Week-End in the Loop," a brilliant article in the 1931 issue of *Fortune* magazine a reporter analyzes in concise detail the banking situation in Chicago in January 1931. Some of the old prominent banks in the Loop, such as the Greenbaum & Sons Banking and Investment Co. had already disappeared through mergers. The five largest banks in the Loop were the First National Bank, the Continental Illinois National Bank, the Foreman-State Bank, the Harris Trust and Savings Bank and the Northern Trust Company. There were also numerous smaller banks, some Jewish owned.

According to the Fortune article, the Foreman Bank, combined with the State Bank, now had many smaller banks outside the Loop demanding large amounts of cash to stave off rumors that the small banks would fail, causing a "run" on the banks by depositors. Apparently, the State Bank had owned many more of these cash-poor banks than did the old Foreman Bank. In any event, Walter Head, the President, is often blamed for adopting a policy of aiding these small banks, thus reducing the liquidity of the Foreman State Bank. But it may be argued in his defense that if he had allowed his subsidiary banks to default, then certainly there would be consequent concern for the Foreman State parent bank. In any case, rumors of bank trouble began to circulate. Two large Loop banks, the Central Trust and the National Bank of the Republic, were forced to merge at this time.

By Thursday, June 4, 1931, a crisis was building at the Foreman State Bank. Depositors were beginning to withdraw their accounts and a "run" on the bank was feared. That evening, representatives of the leading Chicago banks met at the home of Melvin A. Traylor, President of the First National Bank, the oldest and second largest Bank in Chicago. This was at a time when the Federal Reserve System did not yet have the power, the resources, or the membership to act in an emergency. Those powers would not be given to it until 1933 when Franklin D. Roosevelt became President, a bank holiday was ordered and new laws enacted.

Melvin Traylor was the "heavy" in the evening's drama. His price for saving the depositors' money was ownership of the Foreman Bank's assets. The only solution was the merger of the Foreman Bank with a stronger bank, and that meant the First National, since the Continental, the largest bank, did not want to add to its size. The meetings went on for the next two days.

Among those representing the Foreman Bank were Walter Head, Harold Foreman, Albert Lasker and John Hertz. The latter two were substantial Jewish depositors in the bank. Lasker, among other interests, owned the large advertising agency Lord & Thomas and John Hertz was founder of the Yellow Cab Company and had many other interests. Both men were also owners of the Chicago Cubs with William Wrigley, who was a Foreman depositor. Lasker had $2,000,000 on deposit in the bank, which he contributed to the bank's capital to strengthen its holdings. Wrigley and Hertz apparently did the same. But it was useless. The cash demands were so great and the crisis was accelerating at such a pace, that the "Clearing House" chiefs, executives of leading Chicago banks, decided that the Foreman Bank must be taken over in its entirety—and the First National Bank was to be the surviving partner. The *Fortune* article concludes : "Under the circumstances there would be no appeal from the decision, and the bank was indeed doomed. The Foreman Bank was the last large Jewish bank within Chicago. Its collapse meant not only a great blow to the Foreman family and their allies; it also dealt a great blow to the pride of Chicago Jewry. There was a wholly apocryphal anecdote to be heard in various forms in Chicago, an anecdote to the effect that in the final hour of that unforgotten week-end, Albert Lasker said, 'We have just had a performance of the *Merchant of Venice*, and a Christian played Shylock.' Untrue as history, the remark reflects the very natural resentment of the Foreman-State Bank at finding the ground on which for sixty-nine years it had stood; jerked, over Sunday, from beneath its feet."

Under the merger agreement, the First National took over all of the assets, including deposits, of the Foreman Bank, whose shareholders were basically wiped out. In exchange, the First National agreed to honor and guarantee all deposits of the Foreman Bank. On Monday morning, when depositors lined up at the Foreman Bank Building, a sign had been posted informing them that they were now the responsibility of the First National Bank. While some depositors went to the First National to withdraw their money, most were reassured and the panic was averted.

Some blamed Traylor for his tough bargaining in demanding the liquidation of the Foreman Bank equity owners, chiefly the Foreman family and their friends, and believed that Traylor had spread rumors of trouble at the Foreman Bank. But there appears to be no evidence of this. The *Sentinel*, a Chicago Jewish publication, made no such charges, but carried an article in its November 21, 1931, issue advising Americans to remain calm and not panic in the bank crisis. Albert Lasker, himself, who made the "Shylock in reverse" remark, became a director of The First National Bank, and many leading Jewish businesses bank at the First National. It is true, however, that in its hour of need, the Foreman State Bank was denied loans from Chicago banks, which loans might have saved the interests of the Foreman shareholders.

The Foreman family lost the 33 North LaSalle Building. Its banking facilities were taken over by a small Jewish lending institution owned by the Straus family. That bank was called the "American National Bank and Trust Company." Its first President was Lawrence D. Stern, who had been a small shareholder in the Foreman Bank. The Foreman family itself had no interest in the new American National Bank.

The American National Bank was purchased by the First National Bank of Chicago in 1984; it then merged with NBD in 1995 to form First Chicago NBD. Through a series of subsequent mergers, the bank is now known as JP Morgan Chase Bank.

12

Nelson Morris and the Stockyards

Stockyards and markets for the slaughter and distribution of meat developed early in colonial American history. The livestock was transported first by riverboat, and then by the growing number of railroads, to central locations in certain inland cities, first in Cincinnati, known as "Porkopolis," and then, after the Civil War, in Chicago. By the time Chicago attained its leading status, its Union Stockyards were controlled by three entrepreneurs: Phillip Armour, Gustavus Swift, and Nelson Morris. Of this triumvirate, one, Nelson Morris, was Jewish.

Nelson Morris was born Moritz Beisinger in the Black Forest area of Southern Germany on January 21, 1838, near a small town called Hechingen. His son Ira, in his autobiography, *Heritage from My Father*, recalls his father often mentioning the times he drove cattle through the forest at the foothills of the Swiss Alps after their feeding. Raising and trading cattle was a fairly common occupation of rural Jews in Germany.

In 1848, the Beisinger home was destroyed by fire. The family was left penniless when their land was confiscated in the social upheaval that followed the failed Revolution of 1848 in Southern Germany. Moritz's father, intent on providing a better future for his son, managed to finance the boy's emigration, sending him to an uncle, a peddler in New England. His name was changed to Nelson Morris, and his nickname became "Nels."

Nels soon discovered his antipathy to peddling, and he ran away from his uncle's home. Trekking into Pennsylvania, he found work as a coal miner and charcoal burner. He was about 15 years of age at the time. Hearing of better opportunities in the West, he headed in that direction, working his way on a canal boat to Buffalo, New York, and from there on a vessel bound for Chicago. But the captain chose to dock in Michigan City, Indiana, forcing the boy to walk the rest of the way, approximately 65 miles, to Chicago.

Arriving here in 1853, Nelson found a job as a watchman at an old stockyard located at Cottage Grove and 30th Street, managed by John B. Sherman, who later founded the Union Stockyards and Transportation Company. The boy's wages were five dollars per month, plus room and board. At the same time, he also began to trade in cattle. He now had the opportunity to use his skills in the cattle business to accumulate wealth. (Ira explains in his book that young Nelson's drive for money was to buy back his parents' land and rebuild their home in Germany.)

When the American Civil War began in 1861, new prospects arose for the cattle trade. Nelson became closely associated with meatpacker Philip Armour. Nelson won a bid from the Federal government to deliver 20,000 cattle to destinations in cities near the battle zones. He now gained the reputation as an outstanding trader in livestock, and he acquired a slaughterhouse and butcher shop in Chicago at 31st Street at the lakefront. He continued to be an active trader for the Union Army.

At the end of the war in 1865, the stockyards were moved to a permanent location at 45th Street and Halsted. Nelson's stockyard was one of the first to be located there. That site became the location of the principal meat processing plant of Morris & Co. in Chicago. By the end of the 1880s, Morris's facilities consisted of a floor space of 60 acres, 40 buildings, and a daily capacity of 5,000 cattle, 10,000 hogs, 6,000 sheep and 1,000 calves. Nelson also owned extensive plants in East St. Louis, Illinois; South Bend, Indiana; St. Joseph, Michigan; and Kansas City, Missouri. In addition, he had homes and offices in many countries around the world, a huge cattle ranch in Texas, and ranches in other western states. According to *The Encyclopedia of Chicago* (2004, The University of Chicago Press and The Newberry Library): "At the turn of the century, Nelson Morris & Co. had nearly 100 branches across the United States and employed over 3,700 people at the Union Stock Yard. By the time the founder died in 1907, annual sales had reached about $100 million."

In 1863, Nelson was married to Sarah Vogel, a Chicago Jewish woman, after which he built a "simple home" at 25th Street and Indiana Avenue, where the devoted couple lived for the rest of their lives. They had three sons: Edward, Herbert, and Ira, and two daughters: Augusta (who married M.L. Rothschild), and Maude (who married M.C. Schwab).

Despite his lack of formal education, Nelson attained important social and economic positions. He was elected a director of the First National Bank of Chicago in 1872—the first Jew elected to that Board—where he served until his death. He was also director and part owner of the Drovers Bank, which in its early years had its main business from the stockyards.

Ira's book refers to his father spending leisure time at the Standard Club. As for his membership in other Jewish organizations or participation in the religious life of the Jewish community, little is known. He is said to have been one of the founders of Sinai Congregation, but his name seems to have disappeared from the membership rolls. In an undated letter to Ira, Nelson wrote:

"You know my views of organized religion. I have no use for darkness, no fears for the hereafter. Impractical people try to make the ignorant more ignorant and teach them to hate instead of love our government, and hate those who furnish their living."

Obviously, Nelson was a conservative when it came to politics, fearful of labor unions and their threats of strikes and violence. In his personal life, he had a love for horses, and his favorite horse-drawn carriage was his means of transportation. He never drove a car for personal travel and urged his wife never to drive.

In spite of his political conservatism, toward the end of his life, in 1905, he was one of the founders of a settlement house, the Abraham Lincoln Centre, at 38th Street and Cottage Grove Avenue, which still exists at the same location.

Although Nelson traveled a great deal, visiting the Carlsbad Spa in Germany and spending the months of February and March in Santa Barbara, California, he was very attached to his home on Indiana Avenue. No mention is made anywhere of his returning to visit his parents in Hechingen or of their visiting their son in America.

Ira Nelson Morris, the youngest son of Nelson and Sarah, had steadfastly rejected the idea of working in the yards, He managed to attend Yale University for a time despite the strong objections of his domineering father, who wanted all his sons close to him, working together in the business. Ira, in his autobiography, describes in detail the slaughtering and processing of the animals, and of his revulsion at witnessing the scene. Yet he expresses "respect and admiration for the efficiency of these operations and their usefulness to the human race. . . . I had only respect for the business, but I knew I did not belong in it."

Ira had married Lilly Rothschild of New York in 1898, but in the the middle of their wedding trip, they were suddenly called home by the death of his brother Herbert. Ira was obliged to return to work in the management of the family business.

Nelson Morris died on August 27, 1907, in his Chicago home. Cause of death seemed to have been a condition related to "hardening of the arteries." An obituary article in the Chicago Tribune states: "It was [Nelson] Morris who suggested . . . the name of the Abraham Lincoln Centre. He was the main support of that social work, and friends strongly approved of holding his funeral service there." His interment was at Rosehill Cemetery.

Sarah Morris was killed in an automobile accident at Fontainbleau, France, on September 16, 1909.

Further tragedy followed for the family. Edward Morris, Nelson's eldest son, died in 1913. He had worked in the business since his youth and had been given control of Morris & Co. upon the death of his father. He was a defendant in a criminal antitrust suit brought by the U.S. Government against the leading Chicago meatpackers, which alleged that they had taken control of the industry by establishing a cartel. Though the government lost the case, the stress of thc trial was said to have been the indirect cause of Edward's early death.

His widow, Helen Swift Morris, whom he had married in 1871, was the daughter of Gustavus Swift, one of the stockyards' founding triumvirate. Since she was now a principal owner of the Morris & Co. estate as well as the head of Swift & Company, she became one of the wealthiest individuals in America. She got an offer to sell Morris & Co. for $30,000,000, but decided to keep the business for her sons Edward, Jr., and Nelson.

Helen was also left with two much younger daughters, Muriel and Ruth. The sons ran the business, "with considerable help from my mother, a good businesswoman," writes Muriel.

The Morris activities in the stockyards ceased in 1924 when the company was absorbed by Armour..

Ira Morris writes: "Perhaps the most gratifying tasks that I have had have been in helping with some of the details of establishing and carrying on fitting memorials to my father and mother, as arranged in their wills: The Nelson Morris Memorial Institute for Medical Research and the Sarah Morris Hospital for Children, both connected with Michael Reese Hospital of Chicago . . ." Both buildings were erected in 1913, the year of Edward Morris's tragic early death. The Nelson Morris Institute was demolished in 1966. The famous Sarah Morris Hospital, known for its comforts, came down in 1968 after 55 years of service.

Ira Morris began a career in diplomacy in 1914 when he was named Minister to Sweden by President Woodrow Wilson. In his government work Ira was proud to be able to serve five presidents, from Wilson to FDR. He was one of the founders of the Cliff Dwellers' Club in Chicago and associated with prominent figures in the international art community.

As for the patriarch of the family, when Nelson Morris is remembered today it is in connection with the revelations about the Union Stockyards at the turn of the twentieth century—the grim working conditions, the low wages, and the racial strife—all so vividly described by Upton Sinclair in his book, *The Jungle*.

Part III

Culture in the City

13

Meyer Levin and Kibbutz Buchenwald Diary

In 1938, Chicago author Meyer Levin returned to the United States from his travels in Spain and Israel with his wife, the chemist, Mable E. Schamp. who gave birth on June 18, 1938 in suburban Glencoe to Levin's first son, Eli (also now known as Jo Batiste).

With the outbreak of World War II, Levin moved to Hollywood. Initially he worked as a writer on defense projects, then made films for the Office of War Information, and later enlisted in the Army, serving briefly as a propagandist in the Psychological Warfare Division, posted to England. There, in 1943, he met Tereska Torres, whom he had come to know briefly in Paris when she was a young girl and he was studying with her father, the artist Marek Szwarc. Tereska would later become his second wife and the mother of another son, Mikael.

After D-Day, Levin landed in France, and, as an American war correspondent, embarked on a journey through Europe, writing reports carried by many American newspapers and magazines. In his autobiography *In Search* (1950), Levin describes his journey from Paris to Prague, the Battle of the Bulge, and the liberation of the first concentration camps.

Using the same method he employed in writing *Citizens* (1940), the story of the 1937 Memorial Day Massacre in Chicago, he now devoted his energy to the fate of the survivors of the camps and their struggle to emigrate to Palestine. In his initial reaction to entering the camps and seeing the indescribable horror, misery and death, he wrote that his life had been shattered and his mission now was to be a witness to the genocide that had afflicted his people, and to do everything in his power to help the survivors. Among his early projects was the making of two semi-documentary movies. He wrote and directed *My Father's House*, the story of a child who survives the camps and embarks on a journey through Palestine searching for his parents. Another movie, *The Illegals*, was a docu-drama about illegal immigration to Palestine. This movie follows a group of survivors on their perilous journey to Palestine, through Europe, their odyssey across the Mediterranean, and their interception by British naval vessels. Both Levin and Tereska acted in this film.

In addition, one of the early post-war publications about Holocaust survivors was *Kibbutz Buchenwald, Selections from the Kibbutz Diary*, translated and edited by Meyer Levin with illustrations by Ann Neumann, published in 1946 by Lion the Printer, Tel-Aviv for the Zionist Organization Youth Department.

Buchenwald was one of the first concentration camps entered by American troops in April 1945. Levin was the American war correspondent who accompanied them. The camp was located near the German city of Weimar, whose citizens later claimed they knew nothing of the nature of this notorious place, where tens of thousands of Jews and political prisoners died from brutal physical labor, starvation and disease. Among the Buchenwald survivors were young Jews who had survived imprisonment in other camps, and then had been transported to Buchenwald near the end of the war. Levin's shock at the events that had transpired at the camp and the resultant deep pessimism he felt about the future of the Jewish people appears to have been alleviated by his meeting and discussions with these young survivors of Buchenwald.

A number of them had founded a kibbutz, a commune, after their liberation. They had been moved to a farm area near the camp in order to begin their training for life on a kibbutz in Palestine. The young men and women of the commune had decided to keep a diary of the highlights of their commune activities, and the diary came to Levin's attention. He translated it from Yiddish to English and then edited it. In his foreword to the publication, Levin writes that these "Jewish survivors, the first concentration camp survivors to come to Palestine as a unit, provide the answers to many questions that had been debated with a great deal of confusion and very little evidence, by people who have had little or no contact with the facts of concentration camp life."

In their diary, Levin says, "are the answers to such questions as: What sort of people survived in the concentration camps? Are they fit material for life in Palestine? Is there any optimism left in them? How do they feel in relation to their past? Will they be a burden to Palestine? Have they anything to teach us?" To the final question Levin provides his own answer: "I believe they have."

The book makes two very strong points: first, the survivors (now comrades) of Kibbutz Buchenwald were determined to resume a vigorous life; and second, they felt a responsibility to those who did not survive and to themselves never to forget the violence done to them all as Jews. One comrade mourns his "unforgettable ones": his "parents, brothers, sisters, uncles, aunts, cousins." He recalls their deaths, his loneliness and suffering, and his ultimate liberation, wondering why he survived. "Why?" he asks, "For what? Why am I left alive? Is it for myself? For my own being? No, I cannot feel this. In the camp, I wander from one barrack to another, and everywhere I see only Jews. And in them I see my brothers and sisters, and I begin to feel such a closeness to Jews, such a love of Jews and all that is Jewish, that I know that my only home is in this feeling."

Another diary entry records the first meeting between the comrades and the soldiers of the Jewish Brigade, Jewish soldiers from

Palestine in the British Army, who were helping the survivors. It reveals both the determination of the members of the kibbutz to survive as Jews and their feelings of pride in and unity with the men of the brigade: ". . . an army car drove into the yard, and there, instead of the usual American insignia, there was a yellow Star of David on a blue-white field. . . . Shalom! Shalom! thus, the first Palestine Jews to come to our kibbutz greeted us—who wanted only to go there, also to become Palestinians."

The soldiers explained their mission, which was to make contact with Jewish survivors wherever they were, and the comrades learned "that the war might have ended for others, but not for the Jews." They soon learned that after the victory they did not have "that for which we fought; the Jews were still suffering everywhere in Europe and moreover, the world was still intent upon turning us into Poles, Hungarians, Czechs, and nationals of every sort, who had as little to do with being Jewish as they did with the Books of Moses." The *Diary* also includes moving episodes of meetings of survivors with American rabbis, representatives of the Joint Distribution Committee and the World Jewish Congress, and of their attempts to help the survivors reach Palestine.

The *Diary* ends with a description of the new cultural life created by the survivors in their commune. They built a hall which became the "center of this cultural and spiritual life." Here they had copies of Hebrew newspapers and the beginning of a library donated by the Jewish Agency. A Current Events committee was created, and they began to read the Hebrew Bible and other classics and to celebrate the Sabbath and Jewish holidays. An entry in the *Diary* summarizes the feeling of the commune at the end of the initial phase: "This is a general summary of our work until now. There is being born in us a simple, natural orientation to truth, to truth in daily life and a desire for a life full of meaning and truth. Our goal is to grow, and, developing ourselves as Jews, to become responsible chalutzim, and responsible comrades in the kibbutz of Unity."

Levin's *Kibbutz Buchenwald* is one of his shortest books, only 120 pages, while many of his other books are at least five times longer. But it is a powerful work, gathering as it does the written testimony of Holocaust survivors, and making Levin one of the first to present these writings to an English-speaking audience. The work reinvigorated Levin into attempts to deal with the survival of the Jewish people, and the creation of the State of Israel.

Levin often met with the survivors of Buchenwald, who had taken their commune to Israel, to Kibbutz Afikim, located near the Jordan River, where they formed their own autonomous group within the framework of the Israeli kibbutz. Levin himself began a new phase of his life in Israel.

He married Tereska Torres in 1948. It was Tereska who handed Meyer Levin a copy of another Holocaust diary, published in French in 1948, *The Diary of Anne Frank*. Levin would now begin another fateful part of his literary life with his translation of this diary into English and the writing of his version of a play based on the diary.

14

Isaac Rosenfeld: Humboldt Park's Troubled Literary "Golden Boy"

The Humboldt Park neighborhood has produced a number of great Jewish writers, including Saul Bellow and Isaac Rosenfeld. They were members of a group of intellectual boys who attended Tuley High School during the Depression. In 1976 Bellow was awarded the Nobel Prize for Literature. He has won the Pulitzer Prize, three National Book Awards, and many other honors. He has become a cultural icon.

Isaac Rosenfeld was born in Chicago on March 10, 1918. His mother, Miriam, died at 27 when Isaac was just 22 months old. His father, Sam, remarried, but the family tragedies continued. His second wife gave birth to a retarded daughter. After his second wife died, Sam married her much younger sister. They had a volatile relationship, and the marriage almost broke up several times. Young Isaac apparently became emotionally alienated at an early age from his father, who appeared to be rigid and domineering toward his new wife and his young son, Isaac.

The Rosenfeld family lived in an apartment building near Humboldt Park just off Division Street. Saul Bellow lived a few blocks away. Isaac's building was a large, two-story structure, and in addition to Isaac and his immediate family, housed Isaac's grandparents and two unmarried aunts who, with his father, became models for some of the characters in his only published novel *Passage from Home* (1946). In a time of severe unemployment, Sam had a job and was able to provide for the family. He took pride in his son's intellectual achievements, but was overbearing and emotionally unresponsive. Isaac, who suffered from frequent physical ailments, would retreat, alone, to his room and his many books. Alienation also became a central theme of many of his short stories.

Many of the Jews who lived in the Humboldt Park area had come from Eastern Europe. They were secular Yiddish speakers for whom philosophy and politics replaced traditional Jewish religious observance. Ceshinsky's Music and Book Store at 2750 West Division Street was their meeting place. There, they might read and discuss the works of Eliot, Bakunin, and Tolstoy—in Yiddish.

Isaac attended the Sholom Aleichem Yiddish language afternoon School. He is often remembered for a hilarious Yiddish translation of *The Love Song of Alfred Prufrock*, a satire on T.S. Eliot's poem. The poem begins:

Ikh ver alt, ikh ver alt
Un der pupik vert mir kalt.
Zol ikh oyskemen di hor,
Meg ikh oyfesn a flom?
Ikh vel onton vayse hoyzn
Un shpatsirn bay dem yom.
Ikh vel hern di yam-meydn zingen Khad Gadyho.
Ikh vel zey entfern, Borech-abo.

Isaac was considered one of the finest American writers who could write (and be published) both in Yiddish and English. His prose style in his early years has been praised by many "as almost as fine as Isaac Bashevis Singer." In his review of Maurice Samuel's book, *The Humor of Sholom Aleichem* (*Partisan Review* 10, No. 3, 1943), Isaac writes of the intimate connection between Yiddish and "Yiddishkeit," referring to the need that the Yiddish language, in order to thrive, must be part of a vital Jewish culture ("Yiddishkeit"). In a later review of Maurice Samuel's book *Isaac Leib Peretz: The Prince of the Ghetto* (*Partisan Review* 16, No. 2 1949), Isaac praises Peretz's Yiddish works and says that the Polish Jewish community "was exterminated which otherwise would have survived as one of the highest secular cultures of all Europe."

As a youth, Isaac quickly earned a reputation for being precocious and serious, interested in philosophy and politics. In a memoir written after Isaac's death, Bellow told about Rosenfeld "holding forth" on Shopenhauer at Tuley High "with perfect authority and seriousness—a thirteen year old wearing short pants." As a teenager, Isaac (as well as other Tuley High students) was active in the Trotskyite Spartacus Youth League and the Peoples Socialist Youth League. It was not unusual for a young person to express his idealism by joining these organizations in the early 1930's—of course, history would soon change that and make these organizations abhorrent to American society.

After graduating from Tuley High in 1935, Isaac entered the University of Chicago. The University, under the leadership of Robert Maynard Hutchins, was a center of intellectual innovation. As Isaac later wrote in his essay *Life in Chicago*. "Politics was everywhere, in measure, one ate it, drank it, and sleep gave no escape, for it furnished terror to dreams; Hitler, Mussolini, the Moscow Trials, the Spanish Civil War, Stalinism, in short gaps of NRA, WPA and the New Deal, and the approach of inevitable war."

Isaac left home during his college years and lived in cheap boarding houses in Hyde Park, as a sort of rejection of his father's *petit bourgeois* tastes. As he grew older Isaac's living quarters reflected "Bohemian freedom" but soon turned into physical squalor. However, Isaac's student work was brilliant. In addition to his regular studies in philosophy and politics, he wrote fiction and poetry. In 1937 he received the prestigious John Billings Kisk Award for a group of lyric poems. A critic wrote that "two subjects that haunt

Isaac's work first appear here; his interest in Jews and Judaism . . . and the possibility or impossibility of love and community."

Isaac graduated in 1941 from the University of Chicago with an M.A., married Vasiliki Sarantakis, a fellow student, and moved to New York to work on a Ph.D. in logic at N.Y.U. During his first year, he changed his major to the humanities.

It was at this point that his writing career blossomed. His poetry, essays, reviews and short stories were being published in leading magazines. He was also an editor for a time of *The New Republic*. In 1944, the *Partisan Review* had published his story, "The Hand that Fed Me," to great acclaim. In the same year, Saul Bellow had published his first novel, *Dangling Man*. Because the heroes of their stories were "underground men," the two young writers came to be known as "The Chicago Dostoyevskians." Rosenfeld and Bellow were friends, but they were also rivals. Bellow felt at that time that the younger man, Isaac, was besting him in talent and recognition.

By 1945 Isaac and Vasiliki had two children, George and Eleni. That year he won the *Partisan Review*'s Novelette Award for "The Colony," a chapter from a novel he never completed. It is set in a Jewish summer resort in Michigan, based on Schwartz's in Benton Harbor, where he and his father had vacationed. The following year he succeeded in equaling his friend Bellow's accomplishment by getting a novel published.

Passage from Home is a first-person narrative told from the viewpoint of Bernard Miller, an alienated, book-smart, 14-year-old Humboldt Park boy. Bernard a member of a large Jewish family, is attracted to his "strange" aunt Minna, the sister of Bernard's mother who died when he was five years old. The father remarried but cannot tolerate Minna's presence because of a confrontation he had with her after his first wife's death. Bernard "fixes Minna up" with Willy, a Gentile uncle previously married to an aunt from the deceased mother's side of the family. After extensive meetings and encounters, Bernard leaves his father and his home to live with Minna and Willy. His grandfather tells him about some brief moments of "joy" with a Hassidic Rabbi's singing and dancing, but as to Minna and Willy, he finds himself forced to live in their kitchen while they "lie naked" in their bedroom. He learns too much of the sordidness of his aunt's life and returns home, only to discover that his father is dishonest and does not reveal to him the real truth behind Minna's complaints about his behavior after the mother's death. Bernard himself, eager for paternal love, confronts his father with a demand that the truth to be told. He is not even allowed to stay in the house and must pick up his belongings at a nearby store where they have been brought by his stepmother. The truth to be revealed by the father obviously has something to do with a sexual relationship that the father desired or actually had with Minna, and Bernard's problem appears to be that he can't bring himself to tell his father he does not love him. The novel is a highly complex psychological treatment of traumas that affect family relationships and is well worth reading and discussing.

Isaac's family members were the models for some of the characters. There are leavening bits of Yiddish humor, but the hero's deliberate emotional distancing from those around him—written in the existential style of the day—begins to alienate the reader too. Although the novel received good reviews, it did not sell well. It was overshadowed by the popularity of a very different book about family life in the Depression, also narrated by a teenager, the best seller, *A Tree Grows in Brooklyn*, by Betty Smith.

Saul Bellow's next book, *The Victim*, appeared in 1947. Several years later, Bellow wrote *The Adventures of Augie March*, also a coming-of-age story of a young Jewish boy in Chicago. Now the novels of Isaac's long-time friend Bellow were becoming a great success while his own work was a commercial failure. Bellow, in his obituary on Isaac, often writes of "Isaac's" failings, his slovenliness and, from an early age, his "yellow skin" and poor health.

When Isaac's writing dropped off in the late 1940s—Bellow has written that his friend was "severely blocked"—he turned to the theories of the psychiatrist and biophysicist Wilhelm Reich, who seemed to offer an explanation of the link between unreleased sexual energy and neurotic behavior, and even irrational social movements. Reich preached "redemption in the power of the unblocked libido," and invented the orgone box, a device he claimed would restore energy to the person sitting inside it. Though apparently somewhat ambivalent, Isaac built a "bargain basement" orgone box and for several years used his box to question friends about their sexual lives, characterizing them according to Reich's theories. (The box itself can be made of any material, like wood or tin.) For a time Bellow, too, was a Reichian. Both writers eventually gave up on the theory. The orgone box was declared a fraud by the Food and Drug Administration in 1957.

Isaac's second novel *The Enemy*, a Kafkaesque story, was not accepted for publication, and he worked unsuccessfully on a book about Gandhi. Isaac's marriage broke up in 1951, and he left New York.

He went on the University of Minnesota where he remained as a teacher for two years, then returned to teach at the Downtown Center of The University of Chicago. He lived for a time in "slovenly" rooms on Woodlawn Avenue in Hyde Park, then moved to an apartment on Walnut Place. He died there, alone, of a massive heart attack on July 14, 1956. He was 38 years old. He is buried in the Workmen's Circle Cemetery in Waldheim next to the grave of his mother.

Isaac's writing on the Holocaust in the 1940s demonstrates a profound personal identification with the destruction of European Jewry that "undermined and nullified all previous conceptions of man or morality." For him, the new categories were "terror beyond evil" and "joy beyond good." In today's world of terrorism, "terror beyond evil" seems obvious, but "joy beyond good" is more subtle. The latter reflects Isaac's belief that a moment of ecstatic joy—of the kind enjoyed by a Hassidic rabbi—is all that we can expect, rather than the general good we long for.

Some of his essays on Jewish subjects contain harsh criticism of Jewish religious observances. In one essay, he characterized the "kosher" laws as symbolic of sexual taboos; for example, the separation of milk and meat meant the separation of male and female, and was a prohibition against sexual intercourse.

In a review of Abraham Cahan's book *The Rise of David Levinsky* (*Commentary* 14, No. 2 (1952)), Isaac is highly critical of Cahan's main character, an assimilated American Jew, who is "bound to endless yearning after yearning." Isaac says that Jewish and American culture and character share a "similar play on striving and fulfillness," and this made for Jews' "virtually flawless Americanization." This type of incisive analysis earned Isaac recognition in New York's intellectual liberal circles.

His last published essay was "Life In Chicago." It appeared posthumously in the June 1957 issue of *Commentary*. It is a hometown boy's reply to A.J. Liebling, a New Yorker, who had published a series of uncomplimentary articles about Chicago, called "The Second City," in *The New Yorker*. But 1956 was not a great year for our city: Isaac despaired lack of theater, predicted the demise of the new Lyric Opera, and ridiculed the Kimpton regime at the University of Chicago. He did hold out hope for the city's cultural awakening under its newly elected mayor, Richard J. Daley.

The short story "King Solomon," also published posthumously, is one of the last stories Isaac wrote. He portrays the King as an old man living in a slovenly house thinking about his death. He lives in a city that is a cross between Jerusalem and New York's lower East side. He is unmoved by the Queen of Sheba as a middle aged widow. The story ends thus:

> The counselors vouch for it, they swear they have seen the proof. That King Solomon now takes to bed, not with a virgin, as his father, David, did in old age, or even a dancing girl, but with a hot water bottle . . . [I]f there were any rewards, he'd settle for a good night's sleep. But sleep does not come. He hears strange noises in

the apartment, scratching. . . . Mice? He must remember to speak to the caretakers . . . at last he drowses off, to sleep a while. . . .

So, Isaac Rosenfeld went to his eternal rest as a creative and highly talented artist who loved his "Yiddishkeit" and who, with Saul Bellow, helped to shape American Jewish literature, but whose life ended as an American tragedy.

Part IV

Science in the City

15

Leo Strauss at the University of Chicago

From 1949 to 1968 there was a Jewish Professor of Political Philosophy at the University of Chicago who has been called by some the greatest Jewish philosopher since Maimonides. His name was Leo Strauss.

Strauss was born on September 20, 1899 in Kirschhain, a small rural village in the German province of Hesse, near the university city of Marburg. He left Germany in 1932, having received scholarships from the Rockefeller Foundation to study at universities in France and England. He came to the New School for Social Research in New York in 1938, and in 1949 he was invited to join the University of Chicago faculty as a Professor of Political Philosophy, and he remained there until 1968. He died on October 18, 1973.

While Leo Strauss was almost unknown to the general public at the time of his death, his teachings, books and scholarship were very well known throughout prominent academic circles. But suddenly, a quarter of a century after his death, Strauss' name began appearing in national media; there were a plethora of articles, books and a broad range of essays about him. In fact, the literature about Strauss, in addition to his own 14 volumes of collected essays and articles, is so overwhelming and controversial that this article is merely an attempt to give the reader a hint of what Leo Strauss is all about.

In 2003, the United States and its allies invaded Iraq for varied reasons, one of them being the "defense of Western civilization." In that connection many of President Bush's advisors and consultants invoked the teachings of Leo Strauss as justification for the invasion. The *New York Times* reported that President Bush paid a tribute in February 2003 to a group of journalists, politicians, philosophers and policy advisors known, primarily among themselves, as "Straussians." "You are of the best brains in our country!" President Bush declared in a speech at the American Enterprise Institute, "and my government employs about twenty of you." The President was undoubtedly referring to, among others, Paul D. Wolfowitz, the then deputy secretary of defense, his associate Richard N. Perle, and William Kristol, editor of the *Weekly Standard*. These three, together with many other "Straussians," are Jewish.

Many of the "Straussians" had in fact never been students of Strauss. Wolfowitz, for example, studied with Alan Bloom (1930–1992), who had been a student of Strauss and later became a Professor of Philosophy at the University of Chicago. Bloom was famous as the author of a bestselling book, *The Closing of the American Mind: How Higher Education has Failed Democracy and Impoverished the Souls of Today's Students* (1987), with a foreword by Saul Bellow, the Nobel Prize-winning Chicago author. Subsequently, after Bloom's death, Bellow wrote a controversial novel, *Ravelstein*, in which the lead character is based on Bloom. It was Bloom's book that undoubtedly helped to propel Strauss to national prominence. Bloom's book was enthusiastically endorsed by political conservatives; it has often been described as the "popularization" of Strauss's philosophy.

Classic philosophers—Aristotle, Plato and Socrates—are sometimes referred to as "conservatives," and Strauss was an avid student of these philosophers. With the ascendancy of Republicans Reagan and Bush to the Presidency, many of the "Straussians" like Wolfowitz began to use Strauss as the "guru" for their political philosophy, called "neo-conservatism" Consequently these followers of Strauss were called "neo-conservatives" or "neocons."

Often quoting the works of these ancient Greek philosophers, the "neocons" included persons who had been "liberals" for years before they became neocons.

In a *New York Times* article dated June 7, 2003, Professor Jennie Strauss Clay, Strauss's adopted daughter, a professor of classics at the University of Virginia, vigorously protested the use to which her stepfather's philosophy was being put by the neo-conservatives. In that article headlined "The Real Leo Strauss," she wrote that her father "was a teacher, not a right wing guru."

His research as a teacher and scholar was aimed at providing an "understanding of mankind's present predicament; what were its sources and what, if any, were the alternatives?" She wrote that Strauss sought an answer in the writings of the ancient Greek philosophers. His teaching method, Professor Clay wrote, was primarily raising questions with his students—"which is a method they adored." He confronted his students with the question, what is the "good life?"

For Strauss, she wrote, the choice boiled down to life in accordance with "revelation" or life according to "reasoning"—Jerusalem versus Athens—as these alternatives were often called. The vitality of Western tradition, Strauss felt, lay in the invigorating tension between the two. This tension, referred to by Ms. Clay, while brilliantly dealt with by Strauss in his works, has led to many seeming contradictions and inconsistencies in his writings. It has also given rise to the neo-conservatives' tendency to quote Strauss as seeming to support their political position in situations never contemplated by Strauss.

It should be recalled that Strauss was known not only as a prominent political scholar of the ancient Greek philosophers and later philosophers like Hobbes, Locke, Rousseau, and Heidegger, but in Germany, he also studied and wrote about great Jewish thinkers: Maimonides, Spinoza, Mendelsohn and Rosenzweig.

After coming to the University of Chicago, Strauss, in addition to his classroom teachings, regularly lectured on Jewish themes at Hillel House, where many of these lectures are preserved on CDs. His lectures on "Why we Remain as Jews" are classic in themselves.

Strauss was a close friend of Rabbi Maurice Pekarsky, Rabbi of Hillel House during that period, and a man who had a profound influence on many of his students who studied at Hillel. In his lectures, Strauss expressed a profound love for Judaism, its roots and its belief in justice and reasoning. Above all, despite the tensions with Athenian "reasoning," he was committed to his "faith" in Judaism and in his attachment to his ancestors.

As part of his commitment to his Jewish roots, before he was twenty years old, Strauss joined the Zionist movement in Germany, and for a time was a follower of Vladimir Jabotinsky, the founder of the Revisionist party and a militant in the fight for a Jewish homeland in Palestine. This investment in Zionism remained part of Strauss' ideals for the rest of his life.

While at the University of Chicago, Strauss wrote a letter to the conservative magazine *National Review*; it was published in the January 5, 1956, issue. His letter defended the State of Israel against a charge of racism that had been made in an article in the magazine. Strauss said he believed that Israel must be defended against its enemies, that he had taught at the Hebrew University in Jerusalem in 1954–55 so that he could see with his own eyes what Israel was like. "Israel is the only country which as a country is an outpost of the West in the East. Whatever the failings of individuals may be, the spirit of the country as a whole can justly be described in these terms; heroic austerity supported by the nearness of biblical antiquity. A conservative, I take it, is a 'man who believes that everything good is heritage.' I know of no country today in which this belief is stronger and less lethargic than in Israel."

Strauss defends Israeli leaders against the National Review's accusation that they were labor unionists; they laid the foundation of Israel, he said, under the most difficult conditions. "They are pioneers not unionists. They are looked upon by all non-doctrinaires as the national aristocracy of the country, for the same reasons which Americans took up the Pilgrim fathers." Herzl, "the founder of Zionism," Srauss calls "fundamentally a conservative man," and says that "these pioneers had brought back to Judaism their 'spine' and inner freedom, that simple dignity of which only people who remember their heritage and are loyal to their fate, are capable." Political Zionism, says Strauss, "is problematic for obvious reasons. But I can never forget what it achieved as a moral force in an era of complete dissolution [assimilation]. It helped to stem the tide of 'progressive' leveling of venerable, ancestral differences, it fulfilled a conservative function." The letter was signed: "Leo Strauss, Chicago."

This letter is an impressive example of Strauss's thinking at the height of his career in Chicago. A talented writer, highly idealistic, embedded in his "conservative" philosophy. His conservatism is one of preserving the "goodness" of the Jewish past and has little to do with the crassness or vulgarity, as Strauss called it, of everyday politics. Despite his studies of the Greek classics, Strauss retained his pride in his Jewish heritage and the new State of Israel.

It is helpful to learn something of Strauss's life in Germany that laid the groundwork for his later identity and philosophical thinking. There is a "Stambaum" or "Family Tree of the Strauss Family" dated July, 1910, which traces the roots of the family back to the 1600s, where it originated in the small thouand-year-old town of Amonenburg. The Family Tree indicates that early ancestors of Leo Strauss moved to Kirschhain, had a mercantile business and prospered. Jews were scattered in hundreds of these villages in the Province of Hesse, and nearly all were of "sturdy, provincial Orthodoxy," as Professor Ralph Lerner, a student and colleague of Strauss wrote in a memorial article "Leo Strauss (1899–1973)" published in the *American Jewish Year Book, 1976*, (Volume 76, pp. 91–97).

Strauss entered primary school at Kirschhain in 1905, and went to the Gymnasium (high school) in Marburg in 1912. Marburg, located a few kilometers from Kirschhain, was then, as it is today, an important university town, and was the home of Hermann Cohen, a leading German Jewish philosopher. In the Gymnasium Strauss became exposed to German Humanism, popular before World War I. Strauss recalled he read Schopenhauer and Nietzche "on the side." He also became interested in Zionism.

While at the University at Marburg in 1917, he was drafted into the German Army and served as an interpreter in Belgium until the end of World War I. He then attended the universities in Frankfurt and Hamburg, and returned to Marburg where he met Martin Heidegger, who succeeded Hermann Cohen as the most prominent philosopher in Marburg. Strauss finished his thesis and received his Ph.D. from the University of Hamburg in 1920. The so-called Jewish post-war renaissance was in full swing in Germany in the early 1920s, and Strauss met leading philosophers. He became interested in the English philosopher Thomas Hobbes, who soon became a leading subject of his research, dealing with "enlightenment" and "reformation." Strauss came to know Franz Rosenzweig in his *Lehrhaus* (Place of Learning) in Frankfurt, participated in seminars on Maimonides and Hermann Cohen, wrote articles on the Theory of Political Zionism and became a research assistant at the "Academie Fuhr Yudentums" (Academy for Jewish Studies). He wrote his first book *Spinoza's Critique of Religion as the Foundation of his Science in the Bible*. He also published a treatise on Spinoza dedicated to the memory of Rosenzweig.

Strauss also met Martin Buber, Gershom Sholom and Walter Benjamin, all famous German Jewish philosophers. He began researching works on Maimonides, and Moses Mendelssohn as well as Thomas Hobbes. He developed his own method of deciphering classic works as to their "secret" meaning, called esotericism.

He received a Rockefeller Fellowship in 1932 and went to Paris to study medieval Jewish and Islamic Philosophy. Here he married Miriam Bernson Petry, a German Jewish widow with a son, Thomas Petry. While in Paris, Strauss wrote his book on

Maimonides called *Philosophy and Law: Contributions to the Understanding of Maimonedes and his Predecessors*. In the meantime, Gershom Sholom, was attempting to obtain a position for Strauss at the Hebrew University in Jerusalem, despite the fact that Sholom described as "ludicrous," Strauss's theory that "atheism" was a "watchword" of Maimonides and Judaism. But Sholom added, "I admire his ethical stance but regret the obviously conscious and deliberately provoked" controversy sparked by this theory.

Strauss did not receive the Jerusalem appointment and wound up in England in 1935, first at Oxford University and then at Cambridge. There, in 1935, he was able to publish the *Political Philosophy of Thomas Hobbes*, but he had no meaningful job offers from English universities.

In 1936 Strauss visited the United States, and, in 1937, he was appointed a Research Fellow at Columbia University. In 1938 he came to the New School of Social Research as a lecturer in political science. Strauss's wife and stepson managed to come to New York just before the outbreak of World War II.

In 1948 Strauss published his first American book, *On Tyranny*. His fame was beginning to spread among American scholars, and he was invited to the University of Chicago, where he came in the summer of 1948. Hans Morgenthau, who was acting chairman of the Political Science Department that summer "took Strauss over to Chancellor Robert Maynard Hutchins' office and left him there. By the time he came out a half hour later, Strauss was a member of the department of Political Science, a full professor, with a salary more than anybody else in the department was getting." He and his family lived on 60th Street and Ingleside Avenue in University housing. One of his neighbors was Harold Bloom. He began to deliver public lectures and worked on his book *Natural Right and History*, published in 1953. In 1958 he published *Thoughts on Machiavelli*. In 1959 many of his essays were collected and published under the title *What is Political Philosophy? And Other Essays*. In that year he was also appointed the Robert Maynard Hutchins

Distinguished Service Professor of Political Science. *City and Man* was published in 1964. In 1966 he received an honorary doctorate from the Hebrew Union College in Cincinnati for contributions to Jewish thought.

Strauss retired from the University of Chicago on December 31, 1967. Subsequently he lectured at Claremont Men's College in California, St. Johns University, Jamaica, New York and St. John College, in Annapolis. After he left Chicago, he published *Liberalism Ancient and Modern*, and works on Xenophon, Socrates; and Plato.

Having been sickly for a number of years, suffering among other things from cardiac myopathy, on October 18, 1973, Strauss died of pneumonia. He is buried in the cemetery of the Knesseth Israel Synagogue in Annapolis. Psalm 114, which was read at his funeral service, is read as part of the Passover Haggadah service, celebrating the liberation of the Jewish people from slavery in Egypt. It concludes:

> When Israel went forth from Egypt,
> The house of Jacob from a people of strange tongue,
> Judah became His sanctuary,
> Israel, His dominion.
> The sea beheld and fled;
> The Jordan turned back in its course.
> The mountains skipped like rams,
> The hills, like young lambs.
> What ails you, O sea, that you flee,
> Jordan, that you turn back in your course,
> You mountains, that you skip like rams,
> You hills, like young lambs
> Tremble, O earth, at the presence of the Lord,
> At the presence of the God of Jacob,
> Who turns the rock into a pool of water,
> The flint into a flowing mountain."

Leo's father Hugo had died on January 25, 1942, in Kirschhain. Shortly thereafter, Leo's stepmother Johanna and many of his relatives were deported to ghettos in Poland where they all perished with many of their Jewish brethren from neighboring towns and villages as the "Final Solution" reached those German Jews who were still alive. Leo apparently did not know what happened to his family until after the end of the war. Professor Ralph Lerner, in his article on Strauss, notes that, in 1954 while stationed in Giessen with the U.S. Armed Forces, he met Strauss who was on his way to Israel. Strauss had stopped in Germany to visit the grave of his father. It was Strauss's only visit to Germany after the war. He was unlike Hannah Arendt, his colleague at the University of Chicago, who resumed her correspondence with and visits to Heidigger. Strauss did not have much to do with Arendt.

Sigmund Zeisler

Gunther S. Stent

Elizabeth Stein "Self Portrait"

Paris Garters Box Top

Professor Leo Strauss

Nelson Morris and his son Ira

left: Isaac Rosenfeld and his daughter Eleni, 1945

below: Chicago police attacking CIO demonstrators, South Chicago, Memorial Day, 1937

right: Meyer Levin

below: Meyer Levin's drawing,
"The Tree of Ball Shem Tov"

above:
La Pallina
Cigar Box

right: Sherman
Hotel, ca. 1915

Judge Julian W. Mack

Albert Lasker

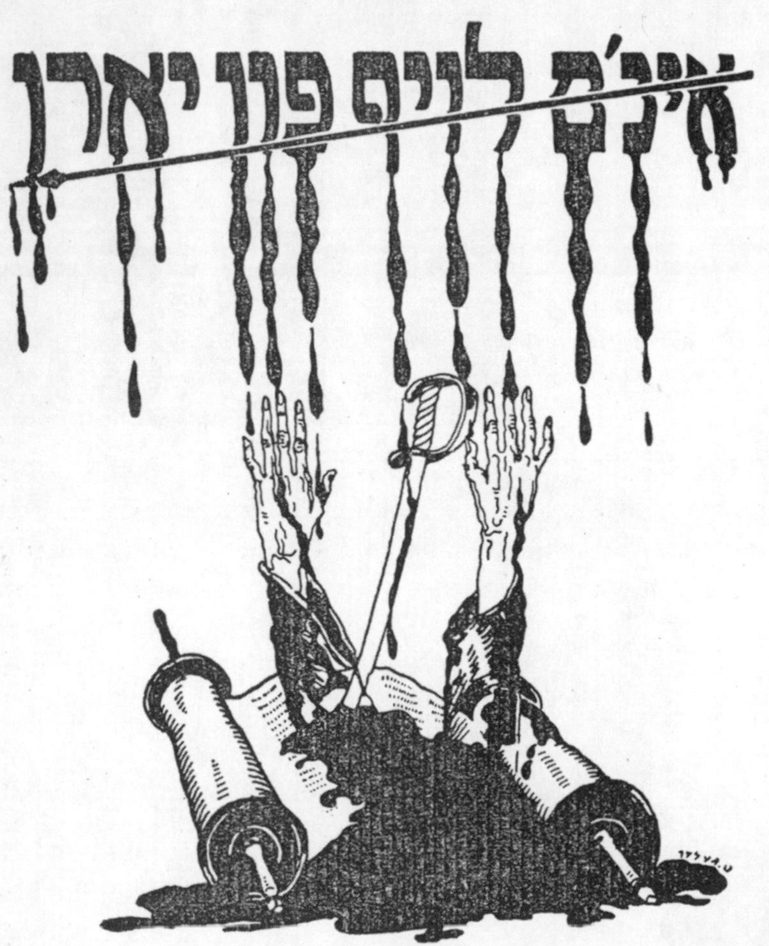

Todros Geller: Graphic for the book *In'm loyf fun yorn* (*In the Course of Years*) by Sholom Schwartzbard

16

Martin D. Kamen: Science and Politics in the Nuclear Age

Great scientific discoveries are often made by young people. Albert Einstein conceived his theory of relativity when he was in his twenties. Another scientist, Martin D. Kamen, who was raised in Chicago's South Side Hyde Park neighborhood, was only 27 when he and a colleague discovered radioactive carbon-14, in 1940, and in so doing "helped lay the foundation for deciphering the chemical processes in plants and animals."

The general public has become familiar with the term "carbon-dating." We hear it used whenever scientists determine the approximate age of an ancient artifact, such as an excavated animal bone or a geological specimen, by the amount of carbon-14 it contains.

Martin Kamen the son of Russian immigrant Aaron Kamenetsky and Lithuanian Goldie Achber, was born on August 27, 1913, in Toronto, Canada, even though his parents had lived in Hyde Park since 1909. His father under the name "Harry Kamen," entered into partnership with the owner of the Hyde Park Studio at 1456 E. 55th Street, and the Kamens moved into quarters above the business. The photography studio was already well-established in Hyde Park, home of the University of Chicago. Many famous artists, journalists and intellectuals sat for Harry Kamen in the half-century until his retirement in the 1960s.

Martin was born in Toronto because at the time of his birth, his father, Harry, had been hospitalized, and his mother Goldie, at the insistence of her sisters, went to Toronto to give birth and be cared for by her family. Mother and son came home to Chicago after three months.

In his autobiography *Radiant Science, Dark Politics: A Memoir of the Nuclear Age* (1985) Martin describes in detail his early years in Hyde Park, the studio where his father photographed his neighbors—a few of whom were Jewish—and all of whom were white. "The only objects of prejudice were the blacks across Cottage Grove Avenue to the West, who were perceived a threat to economic well-being and hopes of future prosperity by the whites in the eastern portion of Hyde Park." This was in about 1920 and still has a familiar ring to it eighty years later. Martin's father's business prospered, and he bought a four-door Buick sedan—a status symbol for the family which only the father was allowed to drive. Martin writes that because of this, he never learned to drive a car. At an early age he could easily read the classics, such as *War and Peace*, and discovered that he "had a strong visual memory and could commit whole pages of whatever I read for instant recall . . ." In other words, he had a photographic memory, a useful tool to say the least.

Martin began his academic career at the age of six at Ray Elementary School, a public school at 56th and Kenwood, that still stands today with the addition of a computer room. Martin's father expected his son to excel in all subjects, and Martin did not disappoint. He was the head of his class. His father also sent him to Hebrew School at Congregation Rodfei Zedek, then located at 54th Place and Greenwood Avenue, and Martin says that the Congregation's Rabbi Benjamin Daskol thought that Martin should become a theologian and supplied the boy with advanced commentaries by ancient Hebrew sages.

Martin had considerable musical talent and soon became a virtuoso violin player. By the age of nine, he was giving "full-fledged" concerts locally. His ability to memorize a page of music soon made him a famous child prodigy on the South Side. His father often took him to concerts. He remembered hearing Pablo Casals at a concert in 1928, "the last one he was to give in the United States for nearly a half century."

At the age of 13, he celebrated his Bar-Mitzvah at Congregation Rodfei Zedek under the tutelage of Cantor Kittay. His Torah portion, which he memorized, was from Isaiah "Arise, shine for the light has come." Martin writes that he found it incomprehensible that with all the Hebrew he had learned, he was not taught to speak the language. On the evening of his Bar Mitzvah, his parents threw a lavish party at Sam Gold's Florentine Room. Cantor Kittay was present and heard Martin play the violin. The boy's amazing sight-reading ability could not disguise his lack of basic technique, so Kittay suggested that Martin be given competent instruction. He recommended Raymond B. Girvin, a leading violin teacher in the city. In his six years at the Girvin Conservatory, Martin met fellow students who would become lifelong friends, and he was exposed to the richness of chamber music.

As his father's portrait business prospered (at least on paper) in the mid-1920s, the family moved to a more luxurious eight-room apartment at 5485 S. Cornell Avenue, in east Hyde Park.

His ambition for a career in music continued as Martin, at the age of 13, entered Hyde Park High School where he became concert-master of the school orchestra. His music teacher was Miss Finley who served the school in that capacity for many years. When she spoke about the orchestra's need for a viola player, Martin taught himself to play that instrument, and he played the viola for the rest of his life with great success. In his later years, he often played chamber music concerts with Isaac Stern.

Martin was able to skip grades and graduated from high school in 1930 at age 17. He took no interest in courses in the humanities or sciences, but loved mathematics and took all the mathematics courses the school offered. Hyde Park High School was known to have a highly competent mathematics faculty; their students won a major share of the math awards offered in citywide competitions. The school's excellent reputation in this area continued for many years.

Martin entered the University of Chicago on a scholarship in the spring of 1930. His original advisor, a Chemistry professor, failed to sell him on science courses, and Martin took the basic Humanities program. He also played viola with a number of amateur chamber groups in Chicago and in various suburbs and outlying communities. On one occasion he traveled with a group to Three Oaks, Michigan, where the guest of honor was the "balladeer none other than Carl Sandburg." His musical activities helped Martin earn extra money to meet his college expenses. The Depression, which had started with the stock market crash in 1929, now affected his father's business, who suggested to Martin that he study chemistry because a chemist "could make millions."

Martin then began courses that would determine his career. The University was noted for its chemistry and geology departments, as well as a Physics Department headed by the "legendary Nobel Laureate Albert A. Michelson." The Physics Department also included Arthur H. Compton, soon to become famous in his own right. The Chemistry Department was headed by Professor Julius Stieglitz, brother of the photographer Alfred Stieglitz. All of these and many others became Martin's teachers and had a great influence on his studies and his work. There were also several young professors who would soon be working with Martin, including David M. Gans. At the same time, Martin continued with his music.

He began to excel in his work, including chemistry courses which he had shunned at first. It was an exhilarating time for Martin. Hutchins, at the age of 30, became President of the University and Mortimer J. Adler, already a famous philosopher, left

Columbia for Chicago. By the summer of 1932, Martin had dropped the Humanities courses and his major became Physical Chemistry, to which he added courses in electricity, magnetism, light, sound and atomic structure.

With the Great Depression gripping the country, many liberal and leftist groups became active at the University. Martin "occasionally attended meetings of organizations, such as the Young Communist League and the Socialist Club and others that found their way onto a list of organizations and groups proscribed by the attorney general in later years." But he says that his "natural disinclination to run with the mob" kept him from being active in these organizations. Nevertheless in later years, Martin's attendance would come to haunt him.

Martin earned a B.S. degree with honors in the Winter quarter 1933 and was elected to Phi Beta Kappa. His next three years would be spent largely at a laboratory at the University, under the Chairman Julius Stieglitz.

In those dark days of the Depression, the graduate students in the Physics and Science Departments were sharply divided in their political views. According to Martin, the "rightists" were found mainly among the organic and inorganic students, "probably because they were still sought after by industry" while the physical chemistry students, who had "less obvious skills" would have a harder time finding jobs. Arguments and conflicts raged among the students. "Meanwhile the roving bands of the American Legion prowled outside looking for communists."

The political conflict between "right" and "left" appeared to affect every facet of studies at the University.

In addition to his graduate work at the University, Martin continued to help his parents with the photography studio, and to play the viola in the University Symphony and in innumerable chamber groups to help meet family expenses. He himself received the Reynolds Fellowship, which paid his tuition along with two hundred dollars per year. His research at the University was concentrated in the areas accumulating significant data on "neutron-proton" scattering.

On September 3, 1935, Martin's mother was killed in a car crash in Michigan. He writes that at her funeral he went through all the rituals but felt that "A spiritual malaise of the legacy of a childhood beset by pressures of being regarded as some kind of scholarly and musical prodigy, had deepened. My experience in academia further reinforced this feeling. I had become deeply attached to Dave Gans, my mentor in graduate research."

With the assistance of Gans' and other professors, Martin completed his doctoral thesis on neutron scattering. He received his Ph.D. in the winter of 1936, three years after admission to graduate school and six years after entering the University as a freshman majoring in English. His thesis was a classic work and set the stage for the next phase of his life. His father gave up his studio, and his aunt and sister left Chicago. "No family ties remained to provide psychological security for me . . ."

At the suggestion of his friend Gans, he accepted an invitation to join the Radiation Laboratory at the University of California in Berkeley. The lab was headed by Ernest O. Lawrence, who within a few years would receive a Nobel Prize in Physics, and was an important figure in the development of the atomic bomb.

Continuing the work that he had done at the University of Chicago, Martin's next (perhaps greatest) achievement, with Sam Ruben, was the discovery of a "long-lived" carbon isotope. The consequences of their discovery are without limit. It was the discovery of Carbon-14, which helped to explain many of the chemical processes in plants and animals. "C-14 also revolutionized archaeology, allowing precise dating of bones and artifacts," says Edwin M. McMillan in his foreword to Martin's autobiography. McMillan comments that Martin and Ruben probably would have received a joint Nobel Prize for their discovery, but unfortunately Ruben shortly suffered a fatal accident while working with phosgene in the lab. As a result, "what might have been a joint [Nobel] award was no longer possible," since the Nobel Prize is never awarded posthumously, though McMillan felt that an award to Martin alone would not have been "inappropriate." Be that as it may, Martin's past was now coming to haunt him.

The Berkeley Radiation Laboratory was closely watched by government security personnel, including the FBI. Martin's "liberal" ideas, personality and religion caused him to be closely watched. In 1944, he was summoned by E.O. Lawrence who told Martin that he had been declared a security risk and was being fired. Martin learned that the government suspected someone of leaking information about "fusion" and the development of the atomic bomb to him, which he was not entitled to know, and also that he had had dinner with two officials from the Soviet Consulate in San Francisco and had handed them certain papers. The Russian officials were Gregory Kheifestz and Gregory Kasparov.

Martin had an explanation for both incidents, the first being that the knowledge of the "fusion" came from his own research and the second was that the Russian diplomats had approached him at a party about whether a product of his isotope research could be helpful to a colleague suffering from leukemia, and it was this information he handed them when they dined together at Bernstein's Fish Grotto in San Francisco.

In *Special Tasks: The Memoirs of an Unwanted Witness—A Soviet Spymaster* (1994). the authors note that according to K.G.B. files the two Russian diplomats were Soviet spies, and included in their book is an "incriminating" picture taken by Manhattan Project security agents, of Martin walking with the two Russians.

For the next decade Martin was subject to vicious rumors and accusations that he had leaked atomic bomb secrets to the Soviets. For a year, all academic and business positions were closed to him and he worked at odd jobs, but in 1945 he was hired by Arthur H. Compton to work in the medical school at St. Louis University. In 1947, he had been invited to the Weizman Institute in Palestine, but at the airport his U.S. passport was seized and revoked. In 1948, the House Un-American Activities Committee, led by Congressman Parnell Thomas, summoned him to testify. He was subsequently "cleared" by the Committee even though it released a report with many disparaging insinuations about his activities. Six years later, after protracted litigation, Martin was able to regain his passport.

In October 1948, the *Chicago Sun-Times*, a liberal newspaper owned at the time by Marshall Field, carried a picture of Martin, unshaven, with a cigarette dangling from his mouth, "looking like a gangster." The picture, captioned "Martin D. Kamen," appeared over an article headlined "Red Faces Contempt Action." The problem was that the article was not about Martin, but about someone named Steve Nelson.

Martin, by this time operating on a short fuse, rushed to Chicago and consulted with his lawyer, Stanley Kaplan. Kaplan said that it was an obvious libel and that Martin should be able to recover a great deal of money as damages. The *Sun-Times* editor offered profuse apologies for the mistake made by his paper, but Martin was unimpressed. But then Martin received calls from the Federation of Atomic Scientists imploring him not to sue because of the *Sun-Times'* willingness "to publish the Federation's handouts." Martin yielded to their request, and accepted a written apology from the Sun-Times in its issue of November 7, 1948.

Martin was now able to return to his research work at Washington University. He published articles and began slowly to regain his scientific reputation. Then in July, 1951, Martin's father sent him copies of articles that had appeared in the *Chicago Tribune* on July 7, 1951, headlined "Atomic Scientist with Russians" over the infamous photograph of Martin and the two Russian diplomats Kheifestz and Kasparov. Senator Hickenlooper of Iowa had released the "spy" picture and named Martin as a source for leaks to the Soviets.

Martin's spirits now collapsed, and he felt that he was a liability to his family and his friends at the University of Chicago and the Mallinckrodt Institute of Radiology at Washington University in St.

Louis. "One black night I reached bottom," he wrote " In a suicidal fit, I made an abortive attempt to do away with myself. [My wife] Beka discovered me lying on the bathroom floor, bleeding from numerous self-inflicted cuts on the face and throat. Fortunately, the knife I had seized had been dull."

Martin survived his suicide attempt and regained his courage. With the encouragement of fellow scientists, he decided to sue the *Tribune* for libel: the story had called him a "spy," who had passed "secret papers." Suit was filed in December 1951 in the District of Columbia against the *Washington Times Herald*, a *Tribune* subsidiary that had also run the story. Washington was considered to be a friendlier venue than Chicago, which was the headquarters of the owner of the *Tribune*, the arch-conservative Colonel Robert R. McCormick.

Martin was now engaged in two lawsuits, one against the State Department because of his passport denial, and the other against the *Tribune*. The Federation of American Scientists came to his aid on the passport case, as did attorneys from the office of Abe Fortas in Washington, D.C.

Martin often came to Chicago during this period for consultations and to visit friends. In one instance, hoping to arrange a settlement he went with a friend to the *Tribune*'s radio station WGN (the "World's Greatest Newspaper") The Colonel himself was there, and the result was what Martin called "A grotesque night." Martin realized that there could be no settlement. The suit went to jury trial and lasted over a month. It was at a time when McCarthyism was rife in the country and the "guillotine was being readied for Oppenheimer, though he did not know it." The reference was to Robert Oppenheimer the famous physicist and one of the developers of the atomic bomb, who Martin had worked with at Berkeley and who soon would be barred from all contact with research on the atomic and hydrogen bombs on the grounds that he was a security risk.

Despite so-called incriminating evidence consisting of letters, pictures and other documents to prove that Martin was a spy for the Soviets, the jury returned a verdict against the *Tribune*, awarding damages of $7,500 to Martin, a considerable amount for the time. The award enabled Martin to pay off his legal costs and to make a down payment on a house in St. Louis, near Washington University. From there he moved to Brandeis University in 1957, where he established the Biochemistry Department. He was one of the founding members of the new branch of the University of California at San Diego, where he was Professor of Chemistry from 1961 to 1978. "His later research focused on large proteins known as cytochromes, which play an important part in photosynthesis for storing energy in metabolism for converting food into energy."

Martin received many honorary degrees, including those from the University of Chicago, University of Illinois, Brandeis University and the Weizmann Institute of Science in Israel. He also received numerous prestigious awards for his scientific research and discoveries. Among these was an award from the Berkeley University Lab in 1996, the very same institution which had summarily fired him a quarter of a century earlier. He continued to teach until his 80s.

Martin died on August 31, 2002 at his home in Santa Barbara, California at age 89. He had been married to Esther Hudson (1938-1941), Beka Doherty, a journalist (1949–1963) and to pathologist Virginia Swanson from 1967 until her death in 1987. He is survived by one son, David, and a grandson.

Martin Kamen was a product of the very best offered by the Hyde Park Chicago Jewish Community. A brilliant student, scientist and musician, he became the discoverer of Carbon-14 and worked with many of the leading figures of the time in biochemistry and nuclear physics. He also ran afoul of the "dark stream" in American history and became the target of the House Un-American Activities Committee, the Passport Division of the State Department and the *Chicago Tribune*. He battled them all to clear his name and in the end to represent a triumph of justice over those that would destroy our liberties.

17

From Berlin to Chicago: "Lucky" Molecular Biologist Gunther Stent

The Chicago Jewish Historical Society is engaged in an oral history project interviewing refugees from Nazi Germany who managed to escape to the United States and many of whom are presently living at the Self-Help Home for the Aged at 908 W. Argyle in Chicago.

In connection with this project, my attention was called to a book by the well-known historian Walter Laqueur, *Generation Exodus: The Fate of Young Jewish Refugees from Nazi Germany* (Brandeis University Press, 1998). Laqueur himself was a young refugee from Germany who managed to reach Palestine. He writes about the adventures of the many young refugees from Germany as they escaped and managed to gain entrance into various countries and start life anew. Laqueur mentions only one young refugee who came to Chicago (though there were quite a number who did so, including this author). His name was Gunther S. Stent.

Never having heard of Mr. Stent, I was trying to discover whether he was still alive, when quite by coincidence, my friend Manfred Steinfeld, himself a well-known German survivor, called me to ask me if I knew of the Laqueur book. I said yes, of course, and in turn asked him whether he knew anything about a Gunther

Stent. Much to my surprise, Steinfeld answered, "Of course I know him, I went to Hyde Park High School with him and worked in a drug store with him at Fifty-Third and Ellis Avenue as a soda jerk." Manny (Steinfeld) had lost contact with Stent but suggested we try the Internet. We located him easily. The University of California-Berkeley website contains a page about him: Gunther S. Stent, Professor Emeritus of Neurobiology, including a long list of his scientific publications. He was a well-known scientist, now living in Berkeley, California.

That same evening, I called Professor Stent, who returned my call the next day. Yes, he was the same Gunther Stent in Laqueur's book; in fact Laqueur was a good friend of his. We talked for a while about his present life. He is a widower, now teaching Philosophy and Ethics at the University of California in Berkeley. He had attended Hyde Park High School on Chicago's south side from 1940 until he graduated, living with his sister who had managed to emigrate from Germany a few years earlier. A most charming man, he told me that he had recently written an autobiography of his early life in Germany and his escape to America. Within a few days, I received a copy of this book from him. It is titled *Nazis, Women and Molecular Biology: Memoirs of a Lucky Self-Hater* (Briones Books, 1998). It makes fascinating reading.

Stent was born in Berlin in 1924, into what he calls a Jewish community very wealthy, highly attuned and assimilated to German culture, and "ashamed" of being Jewish—essentially "self-hating Jews." His father was a successful businessman, and Stent's early education was in rigorous, conservative, Prussian-style boys' schools. He fully absorbed the atmosphere.

He writes: "Soon after the Nazis came to power in January 1933, I began to hate myself for being a Jew." He was envious of the smartly uniformed Hitlerjugend youth group that was, of course, closed to him. Gunther did get to dress up in a uniform the following spring when, at eight years of age, he became the youngest member of the Jewish youth group, Schwarze Fähnlein.

Its leaders "asserted the German Jews' integral membership in the German nation, were virulently anti-Zionist, and glorified Prussian military virtues."

Toward the end of 1934, the Gestapo dissolved the Schwarze Fähnlein. These Jews who thought of themselves as super-German presented "not only an ideological challenge to the Nazi racist doctrine but also an impediment to the speedy cleansing of Germany of Jews." Stent was expelled from the Bismarck Academy and reluctantly faced attendance at the all-Jewish PRIWAKI school.

Much to his surprise, he instantly fell in love with PRIWAKI. The Jewish teachers were young and friendly, the setting was elegant, the students were upper-class and (most important) co-ed. English, French, and Hebrew language studies were emphasized, and Zionism was taken seriously. The students were being well prepared for their inevitable emigration.

His father fled the country in 1938 but Gunther remained in Berlin with his stepmother. His older brother went to London; his sister and her husband left for America. After *Kristallnacht* in November 1938, Gunther escaped to Belgium, living in Antwerp until early 1940, when an American visa finally arrived. He managed to get to England and board one of the few ships still taking passengers to the United States after the outbreak of World War II. He landed in New York and came to Chicago to live with his sister and brother-in-law who had settled in the Hyde Park neighborhood, as did many other German-Jewish refugees.

His chapters of his life as a young refugee in Chicago are of special interest. He remembers his teachers at Hyde Park High School, particularly his English teacher, Mr. Rubovitz, who had a great influence on his writing. And on page 169 of his book, he mentions his night shift as a soda jerk. "My partner was a fellow German Jewish kid at Hyde Park High. In later life, he became a multimillionaire furniture manufacturer." This, of course, was a reference to my friend Manny. Stent says he was soon ready for the "big time" and went to work at one of the busiest soda fountains in

Chicago, Liggett's Drug Store at Chicago Northwestern Railroad Terminal. All his family's wealth was lost in Germany, but he obviously was a young man of great resources. It undoubtedly helped that he spoke fluent English when he arrived in Chicago. He was a superb student, and possessed enormous self-confidence.

He was not drafted immediately, and entered the University of Illinois at Champaign-Urbana, where he quickly caught the attention of his science teachers. At the university, despite his lack of money, he was invited to join TEP, a Jewish fraternity. They needed someone to raise their grade point average. He was surprised to learn that despite the religious segregation in campus housing and social life, American Jewish students were not self-haters. As Stent integrated himself into American life, he coped with his Jewish self-hatred.

He joined the Army and in 1946 returned to Germany and Berlin, this time dressed in an American uniform. In fact, the first chapter of his book is titled "Waking Up in Berlin." His task was to examine German scientific records in various fields and have pertinent material photographed for the U.S. Army. While we now know he was a brilliant scientist, Gunther spends a substantial amount of time pursuing the second word in his book title, "Women." He met a beautiful German actress and began a lengthy affair, the first of a number of affairs. He apparently preserved his correspondence with his various lovers and these are printed at length in the book. Only one of his lovers was Jewish and she rejected him and married a Gentile.

Stent confides to us that in 1968 he had finally managed to overcome his Jewish "self-hatred." He visited Israel in that year and the Israeli victory in the Six-Day War showed him that Jews could fight back and develop as a people, and he was proud of them.

He "discovered science" at the University of Illinois, and it was as a scientist in a U.S. Army uniform that he returned to postwar Germany. By 1948, he was embarked on a career in the new field of molecular biology. His mentor was Max Delbrück. One colleague was James Watson. In 1952, Stent was invited to UC-Berkeley, where during his long tenure, he made fundamental contributions in three distinct areas: molecular biology, neurobiology, and the history and philosophy of science. He edited the Critical Edition of *The Double Helix*, James Watson's fascinating book about the discovery of DNA. By 1950, Gunther had begun the serious part of his career. He met brilliant scientists and worked at various scientific laboratories at Cold Harbor, Long Island and in Copenhagen. He has received many awards for his research in the discovery and decoding of DNA and he has written a number of highly acclaimed scientific books in this area, including *Molecular Biology of Bacterial Viruses, Molecular Genetics, The Coming of the Golden Age* and *Paradoxes of Progress*.

Nazis, Women and Molecular Biology often reads like a novel. Stent describes his youthful relationships with women—his liaisons and love affairs—and includes excerpts of letters to and from his partners (discreetly changing their names). He writes of his interactions with some of the world's greatest scientists, and makes a wry, modest assessment of his own accomplishments.

While his stay in Chicago was only for a relatively short-time in his long life, the education he received at Hyde Park High and his reception in Chicago, made it possible for him to quickly integrate the best values of American society, resulting in the important contributions he has made to his adopted land.

Part V

Avengers and Defenders

18

The Mexican Adventure of Paul Rothenberg

Can you visualize a potential colony of at least 25,000 Jews, to be established in North America in the early 1900's as a refuge for Eastern European Jews, particularly Ukrainians, who needed to flee from pogroms in which tens of thousands of Jews had been killed? Such a colony was the dream of Chicagoan Paul W. Rothenberg.

He was born on August 30, 1884, in Berlad, Romania, the son of Ascher and Beila Saphier Rothenberg. At the age of 4, he came with his parents to America and settled in Chicago, where he attended grammar and high school. A bright student with many interests, he entered the Illinois School of Medicine and graduated from the Department of Chemistry. He also obtained a law degree from the Webster Law School and was admitted to the bar. However, instead of entering scientific or legal professions, he chose a career in politics and "achieved a certain amount of success as one of the leaders of the Republican party." In addition to being prominent in the local political arena, he was employed as an analyst by the State of Illinois from 1909 to 1913, and in 1920 became secretary to the president of the Chicago Sanitary District.

Rothenberg had become well known in the Chicago Lawndale area, a community with a rapidly growing Jewish population. It was the pre-New Deal Era, when a great many Jews voted for the

Republican party which had won control of the U.S. Government with the election of Warren Harding as President in 1920. That year also marked the ascendancy of General Alvaro Obregon as President of Mexico after a tumultuous decade of revolution in that country.

A short recount of Mexican history at this time may be helpful. In 1911, Francisco Madero was elected President of Mexico, after leading a revolt against the administration of Porfirio Diaz, the longtime President, who was forced into exile. By 1913, many groups had become disenchanted with Madero's handling of Mexico's problems, and he was overthrown and killed. Victoriano Huerta, a military leader, was elected President in 1914, but he too, was soon overthrown by four disharmonious revolutionary generals: Emiliano Zapata, Pancho Villa, Venusiano Carranza, and Alvara Obregon. Zapata was the famous peasant leader; Villa is best-known to Americans for his raid into Texas which caused a retaliatory invasion of Mexico by the U.S. Army; Carranza, a more moderate figure, was elected President in 1917 to succeed Huerta; and Obregon became a minister in the Carranza regime.

By 1920, under Carranza, the Mexicans had succeeded in framing a new constitution granting broad rights to the peasantry and limiting the President to a single four-year term. Carranza sought to stay in control by backing a puppet candidate, but the popular Obregon ran against him and won the Presidency.

President Obregon began to seek recognition from the United States, which balked at recognizing the new regime. Years of internal strife, attacks on churches and the leftist tendencies of the revolutionary forces did not, to say the least, help his cause in America. Obregon sent a commission of his officials to various U.S. state legislatures asking them to adopt resolutions urging the U.S. Government to recognize the new Mexican government. Illinois was one of the selected states, and the Mexican representative sought out Paul Rothenberg and explained their mission. Rothenberg agreed to help and succeeded in getting the Illinois legislature to adopt a resolution approving Mexican recognition. Other legislators followed suit and Mexico received U.S. diplomatic recognition.

According to Philip P. Bregstone, in his *Chicago and Its Jews—a Cultural History* (privately published in 1933), soon after this diplomatic recognition, emissaries of the Mexican government came to Rothenberg and "tactfully" offered him a considerable sum of money for his efforts, which he refused. Shortly thereafter, Rothenberg received an official invitation from President Obregon inviting him to Mexico to meet with him and his cabinet.

After missing the official sent to meet him at the border, Rothenberg arrived in Mexico City by train and was escorted from his hotel with full military honors to the palace, where Obregon again offered him money, which he again refused.

But when the President continued to insist on somehow recompensing him, Rothenberg told Obregon about the desperate plight of Jewish people in Eastern Europe, particularly the pogrom victims in the Ukraine, who were looking for refuge in a new home. Rothenberg asked Obregon to consider allocating a tract of land to these Jews for settlement and a new life. Obregon promised to take up the matter with his cabinet. A plan was soon agreed upon and details worked out. "The President," Bregstone says, "offered a large tract of land in the northern part of Baja California and promised that in due time 'he would send him a charter.'"

One can imagine Rothenberg's excitement on his return to Chicago. He organized "The Mexican Jewish Colonization Association" and took a small group of its members to view the specified area. They came back satisfied that it would be appropriate for settlement.

It is interesting to note that in 1922, the United States Senate, at the urgency of Zionist organizations, and over the opposition of certain Reform rabbis, had passed a resolution supporting "the establishment in Palestine of the National Home of the Jewish people." Rothenberg himself belonged to Zionist organizations, but did not foresee a conflict between the creation of a Mexican colony and the Zionist ideal.

Rothenberg then received the following letter from President Obregon (translated from Spanish):

> President of the Republic of Mexico; National Palace, May 10, 1922.
> Mr. Paul Rothenberg, 1630 S. Sawyer Av., Chicago, Ills.
>
> Dear Brother:
> Pursuant to our conversation, in regard to the immigration of Russian Jews to the Republic of Mexico, I am pleased to inform you that the government of which I have the honor of being President, will be happy to witness the immigration; but I deem it advisable to make it clear that if the immigrants are desirous of acquiring real estate in the Republic of Mexico, they must become Mexican citizens. Our laws provide that no foreigner may acquire real estate within a zone eighty miles parallel to the frontier and forty miles to the sea shore.
> We have in our country several million sectors of land that we would yield for colonization purposes. A large portion of this land is exceptionally suitable for agriculture and irrigation. You can be assured that the immigrants we have in mind, on complying with our laws governing the acquisition of property, will receive the guarantee of safety and security that is allotted to all citizens of the Mexican Republic . . ."
>
> With personal regards I am your devoted Obregon.

H.L. Meites, in his 1924 *History of The Jews of Chicago*, writes: "This offer excited interest throughout the Jewish world. The conditions imposed by the Mexican President were favorable, as were also the reports of a committee formed in Chicago by Rothenberg that went to investigate the preferred tract."

Obregon's letter and Rothenberg's estimate of an original settlement of 25,000 Jews, were sent to the American Jewish Congress of which Rabbi Stephen S. Wise was President. They were also sent to Israel Zangwill in London. Zangwill, a popular author and playwright, was the founder, in 1903, of the Jewish Territorialist Organization (ITO), which attempted to locate territory suitable for Jewish settlement wherever land was available. (This followed the rejection by Theodore Herzl of the "British Uganda Program"—an offer of land for Jewish people put to Herzl by the British government at the sixth Zionist Congress that year.

Months of discussion and arguments followed. To Rothenberg's dismay, his plan ran into great difficulty with the Jewish leadership. "Some," Bregstone writes, "because their interest lay in Palestine, and still others, because of their interest in the colonization in Russia, and still others, because of jealousy. There were some who wanted the honor of dealing directly with the Mexican government. Obregon refused. He apparently felt under obligation to Rothenberg and would not deal with anyone else." Thus, the American Jewish Congress dismissed the proposal as not feasible, while Israel Zangwill censured the Congress's leaders and commended Rothenberg.

The American Jewish Congress did in fact send representatives to Mexico to examine the proposed land, as did a number of other Jewish organizations and private wealthy individuals, such as Baron de Hirsch. They rejected a Mexican Jewish colony for many reasons, among them the unsuitability of the area, the poor wages paid to workers, the lack of water, and the superiority of alternative areas under consideration, like Argentina.

After the failure of his settlement plan, Rothenberg no longer played a prominent role on the national scene. In Chicago, his 24th Ward turned Democratic in the 1930's under the leadership of Jacob Arvey. Rothenberg was involved in complicated Republican Party politics.

Obregon had left office after his initial four-year term, as required by the Constitution, but ran again in 1928 after his ally, Plutarco Calles, had served one term, and Obregon was elected once more. But before he could take office, Alvaro Obregon was assassinated in a Mexico City restaurant by a religious fanatic.

Rothenberg continued to be active in the Republican Party during the mayoral election in Chicago, and was an Illinois delegate to the Republican National Conventions in 1936 and 1940. He died on January 20, 1974, in Florida.

Bregstone called his chapter dealing with Rothenberg's Mexican venture, "The Second Ararat that Failed." Mordecai Manuel Noah (1785–1851), a dramatist and statesman, had petitioned the State of New York for a tract of land on Grand Island in the Niagara River near Buffalo, to establish a haven for persecuted European Jews. Noah named his proposed settlement "Ararat" for the mountain where Noah's Ark supposedly landed after the great Flood. Noah's plan failed as Rothenberg's was to fail a century later. In all probability, it was too difficult for one person to succeed in such a project, without the assistance of organizations with influence and money.

California-Mexico-Jewish relations have a long history. A splendid account of the various immigrations to California-Mexico over the years, including a reference to Rothenberg' s Plan is discussed in the article "Jewish Colony in California: Half Century of Hope and Frustration," (*Western States Jewish History* Vol. XX, No. 4, July 1988).

An earlier article focusing exclusively on a review of Jewish immigration to Mexico is *Mexico-Another Promised Land? A Review of Projects for Jewish Colonization in Mexico: 1881–1925* (*American Jewish Historical Quarterly*, Publication of the American Jewish Historical Society, June 1971, Number 4).

19

Sholom Schwartzbard: The Avenger

On October 18, 1927 a trial began in a courtroom of the Palace of Justice in Paris. Sholom Schwartzbard, 39 years of age, a French citizen born in Russia, stood accused of the murder of Simon Petliura, a former general and ruler of the Ukraine in 1919–20.

What had aroused my special interest in this trial was the first chapter in a recent book by Howard M. Sachar, a well-known historian, titled *Dreamland: Europeans and Jews in the Aftermath of the Great War* (Alfred A. Knopp, 2002, pp. 3–19). The first chapter is entitled "Murder Trial in Paris." Sachar notes that after the trial Schwartzbard did not remain in France but finally settled in Chicago, where he eked out a precarious livelihood contributing articles to the Yiddish press and addressing Jewish audiences.

Born in 1886 and raised in Bessarabia (Moravia), Schwartzbard was trained as a watchmaker. He was active, apparently, with anarchist organizations during the failed Russian Revolt of 1905. After the revolt, he moved to France in 1910 and joined the French Foreign Legion in 1914. With the outbreak of World War I, he fought in the French army, was wounded, honorably discharged and moved to Odessa in the Ukraine where revolutionary upheavals were taking place. He soon joined communist or anarchist anti-Tsarist groups, and became active with organizations intent on helping Jewish communities to defend themselves from the onslaught of various armies: Ukrainian (Nationalist), Red (Soviet) and White (Rightist). It was at this time in 1919 that nearly 20 members of Schwartzbard's family were killed in a pogrom allegedly initiated by Simon Petliura, chairman of the Ukrainian National Republic.

After the Soviets won the struggle for the Ukraine, Petliura fled in 1924 to Paris, where Schwartzbard had been living since 1920. Schwartzbard had opened a watch repair shop in the city, published Yiddish poetry and was active in leftist groups, where he met such well-known American Jewish anarchists as Alexander Berkman, Mollie Steimer, Senya Flechin and Emma Goldman.

When he learned that Petliura was in Paris, Schwartzbard became obsessed with the desire to avenge the slaughter of his family, and he began to stalk Petliura. On March 26, 1926, he accosted Petliura in broad daylight on a Paris street, and fired three fatal shots into him, crying. "This, for the pogroms! This for the massacres! This for the victims!" He was arrested and jailed for over a year before he was tried in front of a French jury. The trial lasted nine days and was widely covered by European and American newspapers. The *Chicago Tribune* and the *New York Times* carried banner headlines and lengthy details.

The *Tribune* headlines and brief descriptions of the articles for days of the trial briefly tell the story.

October 19, 1927
HOW HE SLEW GENERAL TO AVENGE JEWS; Assassin's Tale of Hunt Shocks Paris Court.
Schwartzbard testifies that after the civil wars in the Ukraine and the battles between the Ukrainian Nationalists (under Petliura's command), the White Army and Soviet "Reds" and bandit bands in 1917–1920, tens of thousands of Jews had been murdered by the Pogroms. His own family had suffered terribly. He had left the

Ukraine and gone to Paris and learned that Petliura had fled to Paris after the Soviets defeated their rivals.

October 20, 1927
WAVES PISTOL IN COURT TO PAINT PETLIURA'S DEATH; Lawyer Throws Trial Into Turmoil by Actions
Schwartzbard asserts that Petliura was the "butcher of the Ukraine"—he shot him to "avenge the Jewish race." Henri Torres, Schwartzbard's famous attorney, demonstrates how Petliura was shot.

October 21, 1927
CROWD STORMS AS GENERAL'S SLAYER IS TRIED
Former Ukrainian military officers testify for the state and a number of persons, including some well-known anarchists, testify on Schwartzbard's behalf and describe the nature of the pogroms that had taken place.

October 23, 1927
LAWYERS HURL INSULTS AT TRIAL OF "AVENGER"
A great deal ofbellowing and personal insults hurled at Henri Torres about his anarchist past while Torres brilliantly defends himself.

October 25, 1927
PAINTS POGROM'S HORRORS TO SAVE AVENGER OF JEW; Nurse Tells of Streets Littered with Dead
Grisly details of the thousands slain by marauding militias. Over 60,000 were said to have been slain in 1919 while Petliura was in command.

October 26, 1927
TRIAL OF "JEWS' AVENGER" GOES TO JURY TODAY
Various witnesses testify for the defense as to the defendant's "noble" motives and the justice of his cause; among them were

Albert Einstein, Sinclair Lewis, H.G. Wells and Leon Blum [French Socialist Prime Minister].

October 27, 1927
FRENCH JURORS FREE AVENGER OF POGROM DEAD; Crowds Cheer Slayer of Gen. Petliura
After short deliberation, the jury returns a verdict of not guilty on all counts. Crowd goes "wild" with joy while ominous threats emanate from Ukrainians. Under French law, family of murder victim must get an award for damages. Judge awards Petliura's family two francs—one for the wife and one for a child.

Schwartzbard, wife and child quickly leave courtroom and fearing death threats go into hiding.

Professor Saul S. Friedman, the author of *Pogromchik: The Assassination of Simon Petliura—The complete, authoritative story of the Ukrainian pogroms of 1919, their architect and their avenger* (1976), notes that after the acquittal verdict was announced, "Congratulatory messages poured into Paris from every corner of the globe," (p. 344) and that the American Jewish press joined other Jewish (particularly Yiddish-speaking) groups in seeing the verdict "as a new willingness on the part of Gentiles to acknowledge hideous wrongs done to Ukrainian Jews. But Jews also were eager to read into the acquittal of Schwartzbard something that was not there—a pledge that the world would never again permit the mass murder of Jews."

There was good reason for Friedman's opinion. The French press, in particular, denounced the verdict as a miscarriage of the law. Although the *New York Times* and the *Chicago Tribune*, gave the trial full coverage, neither published any editorial opinion at all. Similarly, many secular American Jewish organizations and newspapers seemed to ignore a discussion of the meaning of the verdict.

In constant fear for his life from the many Ukrainian and anti-Semitic "rightist" groups active in Paris, Schwartzbard, urged by

Jewish leaders to leave France, applied to the British for a permit to settle in Palestine. His application was rejected without explanation. In the ensuing years, he made repeated applications to the British for permission to go to Palestine, but was always refused. Finally he agreed to leave for America. Friedman says, "His decision was symptomatic of a sickness in France."

Nothing illustrates this better than the action of another French jury in 1939, which convicted a Polish Jewish youth, Herschel Grynspan, who had shot to death Ernst von Rath, assistant secretary to the German Embassy in Paris, in revenge for the expulsion from Germany by the Nazis of Grynspan's Polish-born parents into a "stateless limbo" where they were forced to live in railroad cars. This assassination served as a convenient excuse in November 1938, for the infamous "Kristallnacht." Despite their looming conflict with Nazi Germany, the French jailed Grynspan for life, and in 1940 after the German victory, the puppet Vichy regime handed him over to the Nazis who transported him to the East where he was killed.

Interestingly, Henri Torres, who had defended Schwartzbard, was also Grynspan's attorney. After the Grynspan trial, Torres, a native-born Frenchman, also had to flee France for the United States. After the war, he returned to France, resumed his legal career, and later became a minister in the DeGaulle government.

Friedman writes that Schwartzbard never "settled" in America, though he lived here at various times and often came to Chicago. A reception for him in New York was advertised in the *New York Times* on May 21, 1934, and he was present at an event in Hollywood. He was working for various Jewish organizations, and writing books and poetry, in Yiddish, about his life, and the Paris trials.

Two of his books *In krig mit zickh aleyn* (*At War with Myself*, 1933) and *In'm loyf fun yorn* (*In the Course of Years*, 1934) were published in Chicago by M. Ceshinsky a publisher of Yiddish books and poems, and owner of a Yiddish bookstore on Division Street. According to one source, the books were underwritten by the Workmen's Circle, a Jewish Socialist organization, which also sponsored many of Schwartzbard's visits to America. There is extant some correspondence from the "Sholom Schwartzbard Arrangement Committee" with an office and officers at 3332 Potomac Avenue, Chicago. Some of this material is available in Chicago at the Asher Library of the Spertus Institute of Jewish Studies. Much of Schwartzbard's written work is in New York in the Tcherikover Archives at the YIVO Institute.

In addition to Sachar, several Jewish encyclopedias cite Chicago as Schwartzbard's place of residence. But extensive research by our Society found no evidence of any permanent residence in Chicago by Schwartzbard, at least under his own name. In addition, it is obvious that he was not welcomed by major Jewish organizations, like the American Jewish Congress and the American Jewish Committee. In all probability, his connection to leftist labor groups, along with the assassination of Petliura and the ensuing trial, alienated many Jews.

Jewish magazines in English, like *The Sentinel* and others, make no mention of any meetings held for Schwartzbard in Chicago, though they undoubtedly occurred. There are letters and oral testimony that he met with Yiddish groups in Chicago, and probably stayed in the homes of Jewish Chicagoans for periods of time. Most of these letters are in Yiddish, but a few by Chicagoans are in English.

Schwartzbard died on March 3, 1938 in Capetown, South Africa, while on a trip working for a Yiddish magazine. He was buried apparently with great reverence and honor for his work on behalf of his people. In accordance with his will, his remains were removed to Israel in 1967 after the Six Day War. His grave is in the "Heroes' Cemetery" in Moshe Avihayil, a collective which is now part of the town of Natanya, Israel, dedicated to the Jews who served in the Jewish Legion in the First World War.

A large gravestone is inscribed with the "heroic" deeds performed by Schwartzbard. The cemetery is also the site of the

Jewish Legions Museum (*Beit Hagedudim*), which tells the stories and displays the pictures of the men buried there, several of whom were from Chicago.

Schwartzbard is now nearly forgotten. His killing of the "butcher of the Ukraine" in 1926, thirteen years before the outbreak of World War II, did for a short time bring to the attention of American Jewry the slaughter of the Jews of the Ukraine. It was a clear warning of what could happen to European Jewry if they did not learn to defend themselves. Schwartzbard spent a great deal of his time in the 1930s, after his acquittal, warning Jews about the danger in Nazi Germany and other places, but the fact that he wrote in Yiddish and was connected with Leftists groups, (though he was not a Communist), probably kept him from being heard by the general public.

Schwartzbard is, however, remembered by the scholar Hannah Arendt in her classic *Eichman in Jerusalem: A Report on the Banality of Evil* (1963). She calls Schwartzbard a "hero," who in the absence of a Jewish state, sought alone to avenge the murder of his people. She quotes from a letter written by Schwartzbard from his prison in Paris in 1927 to his sisters in Odessa (translated from the French):

> Let it be known in the cities and the villages of Balta, Proskouro, Tzcherkass, Ouman, Jitomis . . . bring them this edifying message: the Jewish anger has wrought its vengeance! The blood of the assassin Petlioura, who appeared in the worldly city of Paris, . . . will be remembered of the ferocious crime...committed against the poor and abandoned Jewish people."

Arendt's willingness to understand Schwartzbard's "revenge" motive is interesting in view of her controversial treatment of the Eichmann "show trial" in Jerusalem. That controversy is beyond the scope of this article, but Arendt's reflections on the Schwartzbard trial are pertinent:

"Schwartzbard, who died in 1938, more than ten years before the proclamation of the Jewish State, was not a Zionist, and not a nationalist of any sort; but there is no doubt that he would have welcomed the State of Israel enthusiastically, for no other reason than that it would have provided a tribunal for crimes that had so often gone unpunished. His sense of justice would have been satisfied."

20

Julian M. Mack: Life in Chicago

Julian Mack was probably one of the greatest Jewish judges in American judicial history, although he is virtually forgotten now. Not only was he brilliant, having graduated first in his class at Harvard Law School, but he was a pioneer in civic and social affairs for many years. He is a great model for all those who value public service.

He was born in San Francisco in 1866, but the early part of Julian M. Mack's career was spent mostly in Chicago, and, though in his later years he lived in various Eastern cities, he always retained his Chicago residency, maintaining an apartment at 3500 N. Lake Shore Drive. His maternal grandfather had come from Bavaria, in the early German Jewish immigration to America. After graduating from Harvard Law School in 1887, Mack won a scholarship to study in Germany, and in 1890, he passed the Illinois State Bar Exam. He arrived in Chicago in 1890, at a time when the City was in great ferment: the World's Columbian Exposition was in the planning stages, a new University of Chicago was being built and there was a pioneer social settlement, the Hull House, under the leadership of Jane Addams.

After passing the Illinois Bar, Mack took a job with Julius Rosenthal, whom Mack considered one of the "most esteemed lawyers in

Chicago at that time." Rosenthal was one of the founders of Sinai Congregation, then Chicago's most prestigious Reform temple. Dr. Emil G. Hirsch, the leader of that Congregation, was also a radical leader of the Reform movement in America and an anti-Zionist. Rosenthal disagreed with Hirsch's opposition to a revival of the Jewish state and was a signatory to the "Blackstone Memorial." This document called for an autonomous Jewish state in Palestine as a solution to the problem of the Russian Jews. A few years later, Mack became one of the founders of the American Jewish Committee, also basically anti-Zionist in its approach.

Mack's initial tasks with Rosenthal's firm, while rather menial, brought him into contact with the upper-middle-class German Jews who had settled on the South Side of Chicago. He had the opportunity to work with Julius Rosenthal's son, Lessing, also an attorney, Zach Hofheimer, a Virginia-born Jew of German origin, and Sigmund Zeisler, a Jewish lawyer born in Silesia. Zeisler was married to a brilliant concert pianist, Fanny Bloomfield Zeisler and was one of the main defense attorneys in the Haymarket trial of 1886-87. After a time, Mack formed a law firm with Hofheimer and Zeisler, and did a great deal of legal work for the Columbian Exposition, like the "Moorish Palace" operations and "whether or not the voluptuous dancing girl 'Little Egypt' wore sufficient clothing."

Mack usually handled the written work in these cases, while senior attorneys handled the more interesting court appearances. Mack served as a Professor of Law first at Northwestern University for seven years beginning in 1895, and then at the University of Chicago in various associations until 1940. He was elected a judge of the Circuit Court of Cook County in 1903 and was judge of the new Chicago Juvenile Court from 1904–1907.

An important case involving Mack arose in 1893. A great depression shattered America's economy as the Chicago Fair closed, and many institutions failed. One of them was Herman Schaffner & Co., the city's leading Jewish investment house. On July 3,

1893, Schaffner disappeared, and the *Chicago Daily News* carried the headline: "Schaffner Bank Fails—Friends Hint Suicide and Despair—Herman Disappears—He is Brother-In-Law of Julius Rosenthal."

A few days later, Herman's body was found floating in Lake Michigan. The bankruptcy and suicide rocked Chicago's Jewry and led to a great deal of litigation. Mack became the lead attorney in *Benjamin J. Levy, et al vs. Chicago National Bank* (Illinois Supreme Court, 1895; 158 Ill. 88, 42 N.E. 129), a complex case of an investor attempting to recover some of his assets from the Schaffner collapse.

Mack won the case, but he was dismayed at being the "low man" in his law firm. While he did most of the work, the resulting legal fees went to attorneys more senior to him or more well known. Mack soon left the firm to become a Professor at the new Northwestern Law School in Evanston. In March 1896, he married Jessie Fox in Cincinnati, with Rabbi Emil Hirsch of Chicago officiating, and in 1897 the Mack's only child, Ruth, was born.

Mack and his new family now took up their life in a rented house on South Drexel Boulevard in Chicago, made possible by a "generous gift from Jessie's parents," and located amidst many intellectual German Jews living in the Kenwood-Hyde Park area. He became a key member of the "Book and Play Club," a group which was popular with some of Chicago's leading German Jews: the Rosenwalds, Loebs, Adlers, Rosenthals and others. A wide array of speakers came to the Club: Ben Hecht, Horace M. Kallen, artists like Fanny Bloomfield Zeisler and Vachel Linday, the poet.

In 1902, the University of Chicago (the "Harvard of the West") established its new law school, and Mack left Northwestern for a professorship at the new law school. President Harper at the University of Chicago was also able to coax Joseph Beale, a friend of Mack's from Harvard, to become the first Dean of the Law School. Mack was a great success at the new school; he was part of the inner circle and much admired by his students, among whom were Jerome N. Frank and Harold Ickes.

At this time, Mack became involved in new interests—Jewish social work in particular, and Jewish problems in general. The vast immigration from Russia was beginning, and the depression of 1893 sparked his concern for the welfare of these new immigrants. Mack's speeches and activities impressed the Board of Directors of the United Jewish Charities of Chicago (later renamed the Associated Jewish Charities, still later the Jewish Federation of Chicago), who met at Sinai Temple and elected Mack their Secretary, which meant that he was deeply involved with every aspect of the Jewish immigrant problem. He developed programs for raising funds to help the needs of the new immigrants, and he became a recognized leader in the Chicago Jewish Community.

Friction soon erupted between the new East European immigrants and the older German Jewish community. Mack was a skillful arbitrator on dealings between these groups, with a deep understanding of the "socialist" beliefs of the Russian Jews as contrasted to the rigid philanthropic attitudes of the German Jews. He is quoted in a prophetic statement telling his Jewish audience "Let's not quarrel, the wheel of fortune never stops. Today the German Jew helps the Russian Jew; tomorrow the Russian Jew helps the German Jew." His brilliant negotiating skills and warm personality soon brought him to the attention of Julius Rosenwald, Chicago's leading philanthropist, and Mack became Rosenwald's principal social philosopher on Jewish affairs, though he did not do any personal legal work for Rosenwald. Mack also caught the attention of Chicago politicians, particularly Carter Harrison (the son of the mayor who was assassinated in 1893 just as the World's Fair was ending). Harrison, in order to garner the Jewish vote, offered the position of Chicago Civil Service Commissioner to Mack, a Democrat, who accepted the position to general newspapers acclaim. Mack was now a Professor at the University of Chicago, and a Commissioner.

Within three months, the Democrats slated Mack as a candidate for Judge of the Circuit Court of Cook County. Judges were woefully underpaid at the time, but Mack accepted the challenge, continuing his preference for social service work over more lucrative legal positions. After a spirited campaign, Mack won the election "to the great delight of the Jewish community." Not only was he now "in" at Sinai Temple, but he was a hero to the new Maxwell Street immigrants from Russia. Fresh from the Tsarist regime with its virulent anti-Semitic judges, these immigrants were now in a country with a Jewish judge to help them. Mack did not disappoint them. He handed down stiff sentences, for the first time punishing hoodlums who had been harassing and assaulting Jewish peddlers, and he became involved in many cases involving the abuse of Jewish immigrants, such as the Averbuch Affair of 1908. See *An Accidental Anarchist*, Roth and Kraus (1997).

Mack's prior interest in the Juvenile Court movement in Illinois, under the leadership of Governor Peter Altgeld and Jane Addams, founder of Hull House, led to his assignment to the Court, located across the street from Hull House. Four years as a Judge of that court brought Mack national fame, and he became one of the leading advocates of the Juvenile Court and the child-saving movement which at the time was gaining nationwide support. He spoke to lay groups and conferences of social workers around the country; wrote articles for law reviews and academic journals; and was profiled by popular magazines and in newspaper articles. President Theodore Roosevelt recognized his national leadership when he chose Mack to serve as one of the three vice-chairmen of the famous White House Conference of Dependent Children. Following the Conference, Mack was instrumental in drafting legislation that resulted in the United States Children's Bureau.

Despite his prominent role in the Juvenile Court movement, the Illinois Supreme Court transferred him to a seat on the Illinois Court of Appeals. He objected to this, as did Jane Addams. When his term on the Court of Appeals expired, Mack ran for reelection and won, enhancing his national standing and causing speculation that he would soon be elevated to the Federal Bench. That opportunity came in 1911 when he was appointed to fill a vacancy in the Northern District of Illinois with the creation of the Federal Commerce Court, on which he served until 1913. When the Federal Commerce Court was eliminated, he was appointed to the United States Court of Appeals for the Seventh Circuit, in Chicago. However, judges on the Federal Appeals Court were often transferred, and beginning in 1920 Mack often served on the Court of Appeals in Cincinnati, and later in New York. While he kept his residence in Chicago, his active role in that city decreased, though he continued his affiliation with the University of Chicago Law School and often came to the city for his judicial, teaching and social obligations.

In Chicago, in addition to his judicial and civic activities, Mack also became very active in the Zionist movement. Beginning with his association with Julius Rosenthal in 1890, he, unlike Emil G. Hirsch, the leader of Sinai Temple, had become a strong advocate of the need for a Jewish homeland in Palestine. He fell under the spell of Aaron Aaronson, the Palestinian agronomist and activist, on one of his trips to Chicago to visit Julius Rosenwald, the head of Sears Roebuck & Co, and a well-known philanthropist. By the time of the 1919 Chicago Zionist Organization of America (Z.O.A.) Convention, Mack had been elected President of the first American Jewish Congress, first President of the Z.O.A and chairman of the Committee of Jewish Delegations to the 1919 Paris Peace Conference. He was in Europe at an airport waiting for Aaronson when Aaronson's plane crashed into the English Channel. Mack was deeply shaken by Aaronson's death and he wrote a great deal about that.

Mack subsequently became a major factor in every facet of Zionist life in Chicago. He was a confidant of Supreme Court Justice Louis M. Brandeis, whom Mack had known from his days at Harvard, and who soon became the leader of American Zionism.

After resigning as President of the Z.O.A. in 1921 as a result of a dispute with the Weizmann forces, Mack continued to be active in Jewish organizations, but on a much lesser scale. His duties as a Federal Judge and other public obligations took up a great deal of his time and energies. As a Federal Judge, he handled hundreds of cases, many of them of considerable national importance, such as the famous scandal cases in the Harding administration and complex utility cases in New York.

Mack died on September 5, 1943, in New York. Services were held at the Free Synagogue House, with Mack's close friend Rabbi Steven S. Wise, officiating.

Both Mack and his long-time friend Judge Louis M. Brandeis are memorialized in Israel. The Israeli kibbutz Ramat Ha-Shofet ("Height of the Judge") was named in Mack's honor. It is located near the settlement of Ein Ha Shofet ("Judge's Hill") which had been established earlier in honor of Judge Louis M. Brandeis.

Horace Kallen, in a memorial published in the American Jewish Year Book, Volume 46 (American Jewish Committee), concluded his summary of the life of Julian Mack:

"Take the record of Julian Mack's achievement as a lawyer and a judge, take the tale of his services as a democrat, a public servant, a humanitarian, a Jew and a humanist, and you have a record large enough for half a dozen lives, not only one. Yet throughout the days of his maturity Julian Mack was not a well man. With the most discriminating taste in food and drink, with a knowledgeable zest unusual even in a gourmet, he had to follow a diabetic's regimen, and once or twice suffered illnesses that brought him close to death. Nobody would have known it from him. His life was, through its long last illness, right up to its contracted last moment, one brave, willing affirmation. He took what he had to take, and he stood up, without flinching, saying Yes to life. Thinking of him, one thinks of the words of another great Jew, Baruch Spinoza: 'A free man thinks of nothing less than death, and his wisdom is not a meditation upon death but upon life.' Julian Mack was a free man."

21

Judge Samuel Alschuler of the Seventh Circuit

By the beginning of the twentieth century, Chicago Jewry was the home of a number of attorneys who became leading figures in the American Judiciary. First among them was Judge Julian Mack who became a Judge of the United States Court of Appeals for the Seventh Circuit in 1911. He was followed to the Court by Samuel Alschuler, who was appointed to the position in 1915, making two Jews of German immigrant origin serving on this, one of the most important Federal Courts in the United States. A year after Alschuler's appointment, Louis D. Brandeis, also a child of European born parents, became the first Jewish Justice of the United States Supreme Court.

Samuel Alschuler was born in Chicago on November 20, 1859. His parents and grandparents had left Southern Germany as part of a mass migration of German Jews to America following a series of unsuccessful social revolts in their German states. The family subsequently moved to Aurora (1861), a small town to the West of Chicago, where members of the Alschuler family lived for many years.

The Alschulers had five children. The oldest, Clara, was a teacher in Aurora. Samuel was the second oldest, and the third child, Edward, was active in Illinois Democratic party politics.

George Alexander became the Mayor of Aurora and a member of the Illinois House of Representatives, and became a Judge of the Illinois Court of Claims from 1913-1917. The three brothers remained close throughout the years and often supplied assistance to each other in their various political campaigns. Samuel attended Aurora public schools and had various jobs, some as a laborer and others as a bookkeeper. In 1878 he began his studies in the law offices of A.C. Little, a well known Aurora attorney. During his law clerkship, which he completed in three years, he also did a great deal of studying in the liberal arts. He was admitted to the Illinois Bar in 1887, and immediately began a successful legal practice in Aurora. He was a plaintiff's attorney and developed an excellent reputation with substantial clients. In 1901, he moved to Chicago. In these early years as a lawyer, Samuel also became involved in Democratic party politics. He was known throughout the state as a member of the "liberal" wing of the party and "was in constant contradiction to the boss-controlled Chicago faction." He became close to Peter Altgeld and campaigned for him when Altgeld ran for Governor of Illinois in 1892 as one of the leaders of the "free silver movement" lead by William Jennings Bryan. Altgeld rewarded Samuel's support by appointing him to the State Commission on Claims in 1893. Samuel resigned from this post three years later to successfully run for a seat in the Illinois House of Representatives, of which he was appointed minority leader in 1898. He gained wide applause for leading a fight against Chicago bosses who controlled utilities led by the Yerkes Steel Car line. Though thc Chicago bosses sought to "bestow" on their controlled utilities many benefits by "buying" the votes of state legislators and ultimately won, Alschuler and his friends "waged a losing fight but they gained wide public respect." The fact that Samuel was Jewish may have been a political hindrance in various parts of Illinois to his political ambitions, but because of his wide popularity for honesty and in an attempt to obtain the votes of Jews, who in those years often voted Republican, the Democrats selected him as their candidate for Governor in 1900 against the Republican Richard Yates, a well known son of Chicago's Civil War mayor. Samuel lost the election, but it was close, and he carried Chicago, an unusual occurrence from a Democrat in those early years.

Samuel now returned to the practice of law, and joined the firm of Kraus, Alschuler and Holden. Adolf Kraus was a Democrat and had held various City offices. He also was becoming increasingly active in the Jewish community in Chicago. Both of them were members of the leading Reform Congregations in Chicago. The firm prospered, handling plaintiff cases in jury trials as well as other matters. Samuel worked with another famous Chicago lawyer, Clarence Darrow, on several cases, "including one involving William Randolph Hearst and some of his employees who were charged with contempt of court for ridiculing the opinion of a state court judge in several newspaper cartoons." He also worked on many "pro bono" cases, including work on the reform of Chicago public schools. He continued his activities in the Democratic Party. He campaigned for many Democrats in elections in the early 1900s including those of Henry Horner and Julian Mack in judicial races, Carter Harrison for Mayor and Adlai Stevenson for Governor. He also became a close friend of J. Hamilton Lewis, a flamboyant attorney who was the attorney in defense of Dora Feldman (see "Looking Backward: True Stories of Chicago's Jewish Past" by Walter Roth (Academy Chicago Publishers, 2002)) and a future U.S. Senator who sought Samuel's help in his activities in the Democratic Party.

In 1912, Samuel himself sought the nomination as Governor. Thought he did not win the nomination due to schisms in the Democratic Party and his unwillingness to make deals with the "bosses," Samuel was appointed as Chairman of the Illinois Water Commission, an important position. Though now twice defeated in his gubernatorial goals, he was still a prominent personage in the Democratic Party. With the election of Woodrow Wilson as President, and J. Hamilton Lewis as Senator, Samuel was called upon regularly to give advice on appointments.

Samuel himself, of course, also received opportunities for official Federal appointments. His friend, now Senator Lewis urged positions for him in the U.S. Treasury or Attorney General offices, but he declined these, and instead accepted an appointment by President Wilson to the United States Court of Appeals for the Seventh Circuit, where his friend Julian Mack was already serving, having been moved there from the Commerce Court. He took his seat on October 1, 1915. "It would be natural to compare Judges Alschuler and Mack. Both were well known German Jews who belong to Jewish Reform Congregations (Sinai and K.A.M.). The two men, however, were markedly different. Mack was a Jewish activist, social reformer, and an intellectual who only tangentially became involved in elective politics and the Democratic party. Alschuler was a consummate politician and loyal Democrat who supported progressive reforms within the party organization" (Solomon, "History of the Seventh Circuit 1891–1941"). Alschuler's nephew, Albert Alschuler, the Julius Kreeger Professor of Law and Criminology Emeritus at Northwestern University School of Law, informed this writer that the Judge told President Wilson that he did not deserve his nomination because he did not attend college or law school, but Wilson convinced Alschuler that he had demonstrated his "legal astuteness and his learning."

Like Mack, Alschuler experienced no organized opposition to his nomination. While Mack was an active leader of Zionist organizations and causes, Alschuler played no public role in such organizations. While he stated that he saw the need for a land where persecuted Jews could live safely, he himself kept his efforts on behalf of Zionism a private matter. It is said that "his sympathy for his fellow Jews was strong."

During World War I, in addition to his duties as Federal Judge, Alschuler received the distinction of special legislation which appointed him as special arbiter of labor disputes occurring during the War. His work in this area was on the cutting edge of concessions made by owners to unions and their employees, such as the eight hour work day, health benefits and a raise in wages. His decisions were accepted, often grudgingly, but were considered fair and received the praise of both sides to the controversy and received national acclaim. Of major importance was his ability to settle the bitter disputes raging among packinghouse workers in Chicago, and their employers.

On October 9, 1918, Alschuler was asked to give the main speech at the dedication of a plaque by the Illinois Jewish Historical Society honoring the 100th anniversary of Illinois as a state. The tablet was located on a new Post Office at the corner of Clark and Jackson Boulevard, honoring the founding of Temple K.A.M. which was built on that spot in 1851. (Today the space is occupied by a Federal courthouse and a tablet bearing that legend is still there). Alschuler's speech is set forth in "History of the Jews" by H.L. Meites (1924) and is a poetic expression of his faith in America and the Jewish people. He supported the Balfour Declaration and the future of a Jewish State in Palestine which had recently been announced by the British and referred to his hopes for a future state as a place of refuge for Jews. It was certainly a public display by Alschuler of his identity as a Jew since the meeting of the Illinois Jewish Historical Society was held in his chambers.

In 1922, President Harding, a Republican, appointed Samuel to the Federal Coal Commission. Again, a special law was passed by Congress to enable him to hold this job in addition to his position as a Federal Judge, though he apparently did no major work in this position. He also continued with arbitration activities with the packinghouse workers and their employers, and he continued to gain a wide reputation with the results of his labor arbitrations. An attack on his character suddenly occurred in 1935 when Representative Everett M. Dirksen of Illinois caused an uproar in the House of Representatives demanding the Judge's impeachment in a patent case. Both Democratic and Republican Representatives quickly came to the Judge's defense and "the House cleared him of all charges." But Alschuler was failing in health and resigned from the Federal Bench in 1936.

Alschuler remained single most of his life, only changing that status in 1923, when he married Ella Kahn, daughter of Felix Kahn, a Chicago clothing manufacturer. The couple had no children. Alschuler died on November 10, 1939, at age 80, at his home in Chicago's Hyde Park neighborhood, at 5421 Cornell Avenue. Funeral services were held at the house of his brother, Benjamin, at 146 Grand Avenue, Aurora, Illinois, and his remains were interred at Spring Lake Cemetery in Aurora on November 14, 1939.

22

Terminiello vs. Chicago: The Free Speech Case

One of the most important civil rights cases in American judicial history was decided in 1949: *Terminiello vs. Chicago.*

In the immediate post-World War II era, the attention of the United States Supreme Court turned increasingly to free speech cases in which Communists and religious conflicts came under consideration. The Court resorted to "the balancing argument," that the First Amendment right of free speech "was not to be considered as absolute . . . but rather was to be weighed against the right of the community and state to protect the public welfare."

Lurking in the background were the likes of Gerald L.K. Smith, a notorious anti-Semitic anti-Communist agitator, and others such as a 38-year-old defrocked priest named Arthur Terminiello. Both Smith and Terminiello (following in the footsteps of Father Coughlin, the anti-Semitic bigot of the pre-War period) toured the country delivering hateful attacks on Jews and urging that the United States Constitution be amended to make Zionism illegal. Terminiello also published *The Crusader*, a monthly with an allegedly wide readership. The House Un-American Activities Committee was also beginning its hearings and investigative activities; Gerald L.K. Smith had testified before it and had received a warm welcome.

In 1945, Terminiello was addressing a large audience in Chicago, while outside the hall an unruly crowd protested angrily against the meeting of these bigots. Undaunted, Terminiello made his usual attacks on Jews and other "scum" and accused the Jews of an "organized conspiracy" to inoculate the entire German population with syphilis. Notwithstanding the efforts of a large number of police to preserve order, there were disturbances in the crowd, stones were thrown and windows broken. Terminiello and his cohorts were finally escorted out of the hall by the police. Terminiello was charged with disorderly conduct in violation of a Chicago ordinance forbidding any "breach of the peace," and was convicted after a trial by jury. The penalty was a fine of $100. The verdict was confirmed by both the Illinois Appellate Court and by the Illinois Supreme Court. The U.S. Supreme Court granted the right to appeal.

In *Terminiello vs. Chicago*, the Supreme Court by a narrow 5 to 4 majority applied a "clear and present danger" solution to a case which placed in sharp relief the theoretical conflict between community interest and First Amendment rights. While Terminiello's speech had produced a near-riot, Terminiello's conviction was not based on a physical act by Terminiello or his followers, but by persons in his audience outraged by what he had to say. The case thus posed a basic constitutional question: Could a speaker, himself guilty of no disorder, be punished for an "illegal" breach of the peace on the part of those who objected to ideas he expressed?

By a vote of five to four, the Supreme Court overturned the conviction. The majority opinion, written by Justice William O. Douglas, turned upon a point not even raised in the lower courts—the constitutionality of the Illinois law under which Terminiello had been tried. The trial judge, interpreting the law for the jury, had asserted that it made punishable "speech which stirs the public to anger, invites dispute, brings about a condition of unrest or creates a disturbance." So construed, Douglas said, the law was unconstitutional. The right of free speech, he admitted, was "not absolute," but it could be suppressed only in the face of a "clear and present danger of a serious and substantive evil that rises far above public inconvenience, annoyance and unrest." The opinion made quite clear that Douglas thought it intolerable to punish a person merely because his ideas led to violence on the part of those who resented what he said.

Justice Robert Jackson, writing for the minority, attacked the majority decision for declaring unconstitutional a statute whose validity technically was not at issue before the Court at all. He condemned the majority opinion also for its "doctrinaire" disregard of the discretionary rights of the states in free speech matters. Jackson, who was the American lead prosecutor at the Nuremberg Trials, in particular castigated the majority decision for fulfilling "the most extravagant hopes of left and right totalitarian groups," and warned that the majority had best beware lest its destruction of state police power "turn the Bill of Rights into a suicide pact," stating that this is what had happened in Germany under the Weimar regime where mobs were free to roam the streets because of free speech rights.

It should be noted that in the proceedings before the Supreme Court, Chicago was represented in its brief by attorneys Benjamin S. Adamowski, Joseph F. Grossman, A.A. Pantilis and Harry A. Iseberg.

The American Jewish Congress, then a strong civil rights organization with headquarters in New York and offices in Chicago, filed an *amicus curiae* brief urging the affirmation of Terminiello's conviction. Among the attorneys on the American Jewish Congress brief were William Maslow, a brilliant attorney who died in April 2007; Shad Polier, a son-in-law of Rabbi Stephen S. Wise; and Byron S. Miller, a Chicago attorney who was chief counsel for the American Jewish Congress in Chicago at that time. The American Civil Liberties Union filed a brief as *amicus curiae,* urging reversal of the conviction on the grounds that the Chicago law was a violation of the First Amendment right to free speech.

The precedent set in *Terminiello vs. Chicago* protected Martin Luther King and other civil rights demonstrators in the 1960s in their marches through Chicago's Marquette Park as well as protecting neo-Nazis in their threatened demonstration in 1977–78 in Skokie, in the north suburbs of Chicago. Skokie authorities enacted ordinances barring demonstrations of persons in full Nazi regalia with swastikas. Thousands of Jewish Holocaust survivors lived in Skokie at that time, and they argued vociferously against the neo-Nazi demonstration. As with the *Terminiello* case, the American Civil Liberties Union represented the neo-Nazis, arguing that the Skokie ordinance was unconstitutional. When the case went to trial, the United States Court of Appeals for the 7th Circuit appeared to agree with the American Civil Liberties Union's position.

The Village appealed to the United States Supreme Court, which, in a "terse one sentence order" denied Skokie's request for a temporary stay. When the scheduled date of June 25, 1978 arrived, no member of the neo-Nazi party appeared, and there was no march. So the Skokie case, which had preoccupied the Jewish community for months, was over, although the bitterness and conflict it had generated still exist to this day. Many people resigned from the American Civil Liberties Union because of its representation of the Neo-Nazis in this matter. The American Jewish Congress in Chicago was in a quandary, but basically continued to adhere to the position taken by Justice Jackson in the *Terminiello* case, that in certain instances a community has a right to protect itself.

Part VI

Lovers of Zion

23

Jabotinsky: The Zionist Leader and Ideological Forebear of Today's Likud Party Drew Attention Wherever He Went, Even During His Two Visits to Chicago

Vladimir Ze'ev Jabotinsky, recognized as the ideological ancestor of the Likud Party in Israel, was the founder of Revisionism, a breakaway movement from mainstream Zionism. His image and memory have been shaped and reshaped by events that occurred after his death and by the deeds of those who claimed to be following in his footsteps. Benjamin Netanyahu has been compared to Jabotinsky for his intellect, passion, style, and command of the English language. Jabotinsky proved to be the most significant Zionist leader outside the mainstream Haganah-Labor tradition. His ideological descendants, including Menachem Begin and Netanyahu, have reshaped Israeli politics, and his policies were instrumental in shaping many of Israel's state institutions.

While his visits to Chicago—once in 1926 and again in 1935—were mere stopping-off points for his career, they nevertheless came at crucial moments in a career marked by controversy and accomplishment.

* * *

Jabotinsky's life is recounted in *Lone Wolf*, a work by Professor Shmuel Katz of Jerusalem. Often a polemic for Jabotinsky's views, the two-volume, 1,800 page biography follows Jabotinsky from his birth in 1880 in Odessa, Russia to his death sixty years later in New York. A brilliant student, he left home for Bern and Rome to study law, and at the age of 17 landed a job as the Rome correspondent for an Odessa newspaper, often writing under the pen name "Altalena."

During his stay in Italy, he came under the influence of Italian professors and doctrines of economic theory that were to have a life-long influence on him. After several years he returned to Odessa, having achieved great distinction as a writer. He came back to an anti-Semitic, violent Tsarist Russia.

It was the Kishinev pogrom of 1903 that deeply influenced Jabotinsky and brought him to Zionism. Jabotinsky joined a Jewish self-defense group in Odessa in 1903 when a pogrom appeared imminent there, one of the few places in Russia where Jews fought at that time for their rights. These Zionist activities and his general brilliance soon made him a delegate to the Sixth Zionist Congress in Basle. He became a follower of Theodore Herzl, and by 1914 had emerged as the foremost Zionist lecturer and journalist in Russia.

At the outbreak of World War I, Jabotinsky was employed as a roving correspondent for a leading Moscow liberal daily, while continuing his active role in the Zionist movement. He became convinced that the Turkish empire would collapse and that the Zionist movement should arm itself and abandon its neutral role in determining Middle-East Policy. While in Alexandria, Egypt, he and Joseph Trumpeldor, a fellow Russian Jew and former Russian Army officer, conceived the idea of raising a Jewish legion from the displaced Jewish deportees from Palestine then living in Egypt, to fight with the British against the Turks.

The first Jewish "army," albeit not what Jabotinsky really wanted, was the Zion Mule Corps, which took part in the ill-fated

Gallipoli campaign. Nevertheless, this small Jewish fighting force became the germ from which many of Jabotinsky's later accomplishments grew, such as the founding of the Haganah as a Jewish defense force against the Arabs in 1920 and the idea of a Jewish Army to fight Hitler in the 1930s.

* * *

The founding of the Haganah and its confrontation with Arab rioters led to Jabotinsky's arrest by British authorities, who now occupied Palestine under the mandate of the League of Nations. After world-wide agitation for his release, Jabotinsky left prison in 1921, a hero not only in Palestine, but to Jews in the entire Western world. He joined Chaim Weizmann in a leadership role in the World Zionist movement, and was with Weizmann in 1921 when he wrested control of the American Zionist Organization from the Brandeis group, whose Western ideology differed sharply from the Eastern European views of the Weizmann camp.

Agitating for the restoration of a Jewish legion in Palestine, Jabotinsky quickly became further disillusioned with British rule in Palestine. In spite of their earlier collaboration, Jabotinsky could get no help from Weizmann, who believed in a less belligerent policy vis-a-vis the British. This conflict, together with other disagreements about socialism versus capitalism led to Jabotinsky's resignation from the World Zionist Organization.

Now on his own, he toured the Baltic States and Poland, demanding, in lectures during this period, a return to Herzl's idea of a separate Jewish state, the restoration of the Jewish legion, and a wide political offensive to force England to change its policy and permit the establishment of a Jewish majority in Palestine. He included Transjordan in his definition of "Palestine", and advocated a mass immigration of Jews from Eastern Europe; he predicted a disaster if the Jews remained there.

He also became active in the formation of a new Zionist Party, the World Union of Revisionists. It was in this setting that Jabotinsky made his first trip to Chicago in 1926.

* * *

The occasion was part of a series of 20 lectures in the United States proposed by impresario Sol Hurok. On January 5, 1926 Jabotinsky sailed on the *S.S. France* for New York, primarily to raise money for the Revisionist cause and to attend a Zionist conference. The lectures themselves were peripheral to his fund-raising.

Financially, the American tour appears to have been a failure. Katz, in his book, blames certain American Zionists for undermining the trip. Nathan Straus, the New York philanthropist, had promised $75,000 to the Revisionist cause, but he later wrote Jabotinsky that he thought the idea of a Jewish military group was too "dangerous" and he withdrew his promise. The man who apparently had convinced Straus to withdraw his support was Rabbi Stephen Wise, President of the American Jewish Congress and for many years an important leader of American Zionism. He was to become a bitter enemy of Jabotinsky.

However, Jabotinsky drew large crowds in New York, Detroit, Toronto, Montreal, Philadelphia and, of course, Chicago. His lectures, as in Europe, rested on the premise that the first Zionist requirement was the building of a Jewish majority in Palestine and all the rest followed in logical progression: the demand for the creation of a land reserve, a policy for the protection of private industry, and a military defense unit for the defense of the Jewish national homeland. At first, a number of American leaders of *Bnei Zion*, a Zionist party faction, backed Jabotinsky, but, under pressure from Stephen Wise and other mainstream Zionist leaders, they backed off.

The convention of the Zionist Organization of America was held on June 22, 1926, in New York. After a bitter debate, the majority of the convention backed Jabotinsky's platform. This caused great consternation in the American Zionist ranks, with ominous portents for the future. Jabotinsky felt that if he had stayed a few more months in America he could have gotten control over the Zionist movement here, but unrest overseas compelled him to return to Europe. His impact on American Zionist policy receded and he did not come back to America for nine years.

* * *

Jabotinsky returned to Europe, to throw himself into the Revisionist cause, and to write many books and essays. He was fluent in at least seven languages, a master translator, and had great versatility in Hebrew and English. He translated Edgar Allan Poe into Hebrew and created and published the first World Atlas in Hebrew. In 1928 he returned to Palestine, becoming editor of a Hebrew daily in Jerusalem, while at the same time continuing his agitation for Jewish majority rule in Palestine. In 1930, while he was on a trip to South Africa, the British canceled his return visit and barred him from entering Palestine. He was never able to return to Palestine in his lifetime.

He continued his lectures in many countries, drawing attention to his disagreements with Zionist political and economic policies in Palestine, including the socialist labor policy of the Ben-Gurion Labor movement. His relationship with labor circles in Palestine grew increasingly strained: he was charged with "militarism," "enmity to labor" and even "Fascist leanings."

After Hitler's rise to power in 1933, Jabotinsky advocated a total boycott of Germany by the Jewish people and opposed the "Transfer Agreement" negotiated by the Jewish Agency with Germany. This controversial Agreement was made to permit immigration of a limited number of German Jews to Palestine in exchange for the transfer of their assets to accounts which would purchase German goods. Jabotinsky further widened the gap between himself and the Zionist leadership in Palestine by opposing the Transfer Agreement.

When Chaim Arlosoroff, a labor leader who had negotiated the Transfer Agreement, was murdered in Tel Aviv, members of the labor movement in Palestine held Jabotinsky responsible for this heinous act. Jabotinsky vigorously denounced the act and denied any knowledge of it. In an attempt to alleviate the tension between Revisionism and Labor, Ben-Gurion and Jabotinsky negotiated agreements in 1934 to settle their differences and avoid the factionalizing of the World Zionist Organization.

⋆⋆⋆

Thinking that the internal conflicts were sufficiently resolved for the Zionist movement to face the Nazi common enemy, Jabotinsky came to the United States in January 1935 at the invitation of some of his American supporters. A long article welcoming Jabotinsky to America appeared in Chicago's *The Sentinel* on January 24, 1935. On March 21, 1935, *The Sentinel* wrote that Jabotinsky was slated to lecture on "New Deal for Jewish Life in Palestine" on March 27 in Orchestra Hall. *The Sentinel* noted:

"Fighting for years in the face of the greatest odds, without, as well as within, the Jewish fold, he continues to stand his ground in upholding uncompromisingly maximum Jewish rights in Palestine, and for that reason he is certain of a deliriously enthusiastic reception by his host of followers wherever he goes. He was last here ten years ago. Elaborate preparations have been made for his present visit."

A week later, *The Sentinel* announced that Jabotinsky was also speaking on March 28 at Anshe Sholom Synagogue at Polk and Independence Avenues. During his visit in Chicago, Jabotinsky stayed at the LaSalle Hotel at Madison and LaSalle Streets. A letter obtained from the Jabotinsky Institute in Tel Aviv was written on the hotel's stationery at that time. This letter is written in Ladino and bears Jabotinsky's signature.

* * *

While Jabotinsky was warmly welcomed on his American speaking tour by large crowds, his relationship with mainstream Zionism grew worse. His accord with Ben-Gurion was rejected by the Labor Movement both in Palestine and in America. Rabbi Stephen Wise led a vigorous campaign to impugn Jabotinsky's policies. The Zionist organization demanded "full discipline" for its policies, which Jabotinsky refused. In this acrimonious atmosphere, Jabotinsky and the Revisionist movement soon cut all ties with the World Zionist Organization. He returned to Europe, formed new organizations, and agitated for mass Jewish immigration to Palestine.

He and his followers forcefully supported "illegal" immigration to Palestine and a part of his organization soon evolved into the *Irgun Zeva'i Le'ummi* (the predecessor of Likud), which advocated violent retaliation against the Arab population.

With the outbreak of World War II (which he did not foresee), Jabotinsky sailed for America in February 1940 to enlist Jewish and non-Jewish support for his plans for a Jewish Army. Then in August, 1940 during a visit to the Betar (Youth Group) Summer Camp near New York City he died suddenly of a heart attack.

In a letter in the 1930s Jabotinsky had written: "My remains will be transferred [to Erez Israel] only on the instructions of a Jewish Government." Twenty-five years after his death, with the approach of the Six-Day War, his remains, together with those of his wife, were taken to Israel by a Jewish government decision and buried in a state funeral on Mount Herzl.

* * *

When Jabotinsky died he left a young Palestinian follower in America, Peter Bergson, a.k.a. Hillel Kook. With America's entry into World War II, Bergson often came to Chicago and with the writer Ben Hecht, of Chicago fame, helped to stage pageants and to agitate for the creation of a Jewish army in Europe or the Middle East to fight the Nazis. They were vigorously opposed again by Rabbi Stephen Wise and the Zionist Organization of America.

After the end of World War II and the outbreak of hostility with the Arabs, Ben Hecht assisted in the purchase of a ship to bring arms to Irgun followers in Tel-Aviv to help them fight the Arabs. The ship was fired on by Haganah troops acting under orders of Ben-Gurion, who demanded that their arms be turned over to the new Jewish state and not used by the Irgun as a separate army. Many were killed and the boat sank. The boat bore the name of "Altalena," Jabotinsky's pen-name. Even though he had been dead for almost a decade, the internal conflicts within Zionism had carried on after his death. They do so to this day.

Part VII

Addenda: Author's Messages to the Chicago Jewish Historical Society 2003–2007

24

Dr. Edward Hirsch Levi: The Greatest Lawyer of His Time

A memorial service for Dr. Edward Hirsch Levi, was held on Thursday April 6, 2000 at Rockefeller Chapel of the University of Chicago. Dr. Levi had died on March 7 of that year. The imposing Chapel was filled with an overflowing crowd. Among the many local and national dignitaries present who participated in the memorial service were Hugo Sonnenschein, President of the University of Chicago; Bernard D. Meltzer, Professor Emeritus of the University of Chicago Law School and Levi's brother-in-law; former President Gerald R. Ford, who had appointed Levi Attorney General of the United States in the aftermath of the Nixon-Watergate scandal; Katherine Graham, former owner and publisher of the *Washington Post* and a stalwart supporter of Levi; Justice Antonia Scalia, the United States Supreme Court Justice and former student of Levi; and Gerhard Casper, former Dean of the University of Chicago Law School and former President of Stanford University.

Rabbi Michael Sternfield of Chicago's Sinai Congregation concluded the memorial services by recalling Levi's roots. His grandfather, Rabbi Emil Gustav Hirsch, came to Chicago in 1880 and assumed the pulpit at Chicago's Sinai Congregation which he held for 42 years until his death. He was a renowned scholar, teacher, and a leader of the American Jewish Reform movement. Rabbi Hirsch's daughter, Elsa, married Rabbi Gerson B. Levi of Temple Sholom who had come to Chicago from Scotland; they were Edward's parents.

Edward H. Levi was born in Chicago on June 26, 1911. He was a Hyde Parker for most of his life, attended the University of Chicago Laboratory School, the College and the Law School. He became a Professor at the Law School, its first Jewish Dean and the first Jewish President of a leading American University.

He was without doubt a great teacher, his courses on antitrust laws were classic and his basic work "An Introduction to Legal Reading" is still the teaching guide in many Law Schools to this date. Without a doubt, he was a great American scholar, the best that America had to offer. Not only was he a "Great Jew" as the Rabbi Sternfield stated, he was also a Great American. In an editorial in the Wall Street Journal, Robert H. Bork, a student of Levi and former Solicitor General of the United States, called him the "Greatest Lawyer of His Time."

25

"Is Jerusalem Burning?" Myth, Memory and the Battle of Latrun

At an Israel Film Festival in Spring, 2001, Chuck Olin, a native Chicagoan, received the Festival's Visionary Award 2001 during the Gala Night Festivities held at the Landmark Century Centre Cinema. The award was in recognition for the documentaries produced by Olin and his production company in the past and for the film shown at the Festival entitled *Is Jerusalem Burning? Myth, Memory and the Battle of Latrun*.

Olin's family has deep roots in the business and philanthropic history of American and Chicago Jewry. Olin himself, after graduation from Harvard, began his career in Chicago in late 1960 co-producing award-winning documentaries about social unrest in America and elsewhere, including the riots in Chicago during the 1968 Democratic Convention. Film clips from these documentaries were shown at the Gala Night. Several years before *Latrun* Olin had produced his most ambitious and probably best known documentary, *In our Hands*, a full length film that tells the story of the heroism and exploits of the Jewish Brigade, the only all-Jewish fighting unit during World War II, which was organized in Palestine and fought with the British Army in Europe. The film was widely shown in Chicago and warmly received.

This was not to be the case for Olin's film shown at the Festival. At the screening and discussions that followed it, "Latrun" was attacked for some of the views expressed by certain Israeli historians and military officers for their comments with respect to the battle. One Chicago Jewish publication bitterly attacked the film as a one-sided political criticism of Israel's leadership at the time of Israel's War of Independence in 1948.

For those involved in the telling of history whether by written, audio or visual means, Olin's film is a reminder of how quickly facts can become memories producing myths that later obscure the facts.

Olin's documentary was apparently commissioned by an Israeli general who was a commander of the forces that attacked Latrun. The film begins with sweeping views of the Judean hills, and we are quickly told that it is set in 1948 and that the Arab Legion from Jordan has occupied Latrun, consisting of a British fort and other buildings, and has succeeded in blocking the main and only road to Jerusalem, which was now isolated, besieged and starving. A United Nations dictated armistice date was looming and if the Israelis had no access to Jerusalem, the city would fall into the hands of the Arabs, a calamity for Jewish aspirations for the newly created state. Under these circumstances, Prime Minister Ben Gurion of Israel, had given orders that Latrun must be attacked and captured. Many of his military advisors, including Yigdal Yadin, Jewish commander of the Haganah, urged him not to attack since the Arab Legion was too deeply entrenched and warned him that Arab attacks from Egypt and Syria were perhaps a more serious threat. But Ben Gurion ordered the attacks, and in desperation, newly arrived survivors from the concentration camps of Europe are shipped to Latrun, ill equipped and poorly trained. Olin's interviewees graphically tell their story of tragic errors and of the defeats that follow. After several attacks, the Latrun battle was lost. Some of the historians in the film are so-called "revisionist" historians deeply critical of many of the founders of Israel and the "myths" surrounding their accomplishments. Particularly at the end of the film in a somewhat lengthy polemic, the film enters a treacherous area of the implications arising from past "myths" and their use to justify decisions by present government. Olin makes a heroic effort to present the competing myths. Does he obscure the facts in the process? You will have to view this worthwhile film and make your own decision.

Shortly after the battle for Latrun was over, a small unpaved path was located several miles nearby Latrun, bypassing the main blockade, and this road, after a herculean construction crew did its work, opened a new road called the "Burma Road." Jerusalem was saved and the New City was declared by the U.N. to belong to Israel. It is said that the battle of Latrun was really not lost since it led to the building of this new road. Is that a fact or a myth? The use of survivors in the battle continues to be a contentious matter in Israel. Some say hundreds of survivors were killed in the battle, but that may be a myth for Olin's research indicates that less than 100 survivors were killed. The facts surrounding the role of the survivors appears to have been overwhelmed by the myths generated by facts and memories.

Whatever the politics now embroiling Israel, Olin's documentary film "Latrun" is a masterful work of art on the difficulties encountered in historical presentations.

26

Daniel Barenboim Workshop in the Middle East

On Tuesday evening, July 31, 2001, the West-East Divan Orchestra performed at the Chicago Symphony Center, with Daniel Barenboim, conductor of the Chicago Symphony Orchestra, conducting. It had been doubtful all Spring whether this program would go on as planned given the grave political situation prevailing in the Middle East. Barenboim (embroiled in his own controversy in Israel in the weeks preceding the July 31st event with the playing of a work by Richard Wagner contrary to the express wishes of Israeli governing bodies) created the West-East Divan Orchestra out of a Workshop for young musicians which he founded in 1999.

The Workshop brought together some seventy young, gifted musicians from Israel, Egypt, Jordan, Lebanon, the Palestinian territories and Germany. The Workshop was to realize Barenboim's desire to work with gifted young musicians from these politically embroiled countries with a vision of "building bridges through music." As Barenboim stated in his opening remarks to the Tuesday evening audience, he is convinced that "music has the power to foster connections, encouraging tolerance and greater understanding between people." He remarked that he was aware that the Workshop and its music might not have any political influence, and he said it was not meant to have any, but nevertheless the comradeship and associations made by the young participants in their two week Workshop and culminating recitals could not help but create a friendly spirit.

This was the first time that the Workshop had come to Chicago and its first performance in the United States. In two previous years the Workshop had taken place in Weimar, Germany with great success. The Workshop itself took place in collaboration with the Northwestern University School of Music at the Evanston campus.

The program for the Tuesday evening performance was highlighted by a recital of Mozart's "Concert from Three Pianos in E Major," K.242, with Daniel Barenboim, Saleem Abboud-Ashkar (an Arab musician living in Israel) and Shai Wosner (a Jewish-Israeli native), as the three soloists, followed without intermission by Beethoven Symphony No. 3 in E-Flat Major, Op. 55 (Eroica).

After these two splendid renditions, the audience rose en masse for thunderous applause for Barenboim and his young musicians. After numerous curtain calls, Barenboim yielded and led the orchestra in an encore piece of Rossini's "Overture to the Barber of Seville." Great applause followed again, but the music for the evening was over. The audience, as far as I could tell, approved of the evening despite all the swirling violence in the Middle East. One could tell that the young musicians played together with great enthusiasm and afterwards mixed in social conversations. Whether adult Israelis and Arabs did likewise, was not clear, though most assuredly many were in the audience.

One evening of music does not create any political peace, as Maestro Barenboim correctly stated. But for an evening, it gave the audience an uplifting feeling.

27

1001 Afternoons in Chicago

Ben Hecht was a prodigious writer in his early professional journalistic career in Chicago. That career lasted until 1924 when he left the city for New York and later Hollywood. In his early years in Chicago, he was a whirlwind reporter, writing stories and anecdotes galore in the columns of the *Chicago Daily News*. He had a vivid imagination and could develop a simple tale into an awesome tragedy or sardonic comedy. In June of 1921 he wrote a column for the *Chicago Daily News* of a Chicago story and continued with such a column every day until October of 1922. The column was headed "1001 Afternoons in Chicago."

"1001 Afternoons in Chicago" was adapted for a play by Paul Peditto, and was performed in November and December 2001, by the Prop Theater Company at a new theater location at 66 E. Randolph Street called Storefront Theatre.

The Play enacts a number of Hecht's columns and includes incidents from Hecht's life from his other writings. The play depicts scenes as Hecht saw Chicago lives in action, with all of its dynamics and tragedies in the taverns, the Hobo clubs and Chicago's seamy streets. The Play is a harbinger of the great success Hecht would enjoy later when he co-authored such important plays as "Front Page" and "Twentieth Century." In the instant play Hecht's protagonist is Sherwood Anderson, who had already achieved fame as a writer, but whose cynical and often untrustworthy advice irritated Hecht to no end, though Hecht himself could hold his own when it came to cynicism. Hecht was a 27 years old genius at the time the play takes place. His Jewish parents had come from Racine, Wisconsin to live on the West side of Chicago. But while he loved his mother, he had no use for the orthodox traditions and "ghetto" behavior of East European Jews. He later married a gentile woman, divorced her and then married a Jewish woman, who he adored and who, it is said, brought him back to the Jewish community in "the 1930's" when he became a leading propagandist for the Revisionist Zionists and the struggle to save the Jews of Europe from Nazism and the creation of the State of Israel.

The Play deals largely with Hecht's relationship with young women. It evolves around a young woman that Hecht helped to climb out of "poverty" and helps her to meet a better class of people. He falls in love with her, intends to marry her, only to be told by his "friend" Sherwood Anderson that his love had been a "whore" which she had not revealed to Hecht. Hecht breaks off the relationship but his friendship with Anderson is over. One of Hecht's columns deals with a story of a similar nature, as does his autobiography *Child of the Century* (Simon and Schuster, 1954).

Another anecdote from Hecht's column becomes one of the moving scenes in the Play. Hecht and Anderson are having one of their lively discussions of life in Chicago and incidents that they have witnessed. The Tavern waiter comes over to tell them that Sam, a stranger, sitting alone in a corner, has offered to buy drinks for them and everyone else in the place. Hecht is intrigued and asks Sam to join them. Sam tells him he is a businessman, but that things are looking up and that he has $700, which he wants to spend on his friends, since he is happy at the turn of events. Hecht and Anderson think it peculiar but join in the free drinks. Sam leaves happily. In a subsequent scene, the next morning, Anderson phones Hecht and tells him he just read an obituary to the effect that

Sam's body has been found in a drainage canal, and that Sam had committed suicide. Sam left a note that his business was bankrupt and that he could not go on living. The story is a typical Hecht theme—goodness and tragedy often intermix.

Another scene draws on Hecht's columns about life in the circus. The Great Salvini comes to Hecht to complain how his young wife is so unhappy. He tells Hecht she was beautiful and slim and a perfect partner for his circus act, which was to throw knives around her slim figure as she stood as a target against a wall while the audience gawked. He had assumed she loved him to use her for his target, but lately she had grown fat and was very unhappy and crying in her room. The Great Salvini can't understand why she is doing this and one day a knife thrown by him pierces her arm drawing blood. Salvini is upset, tells Hecht he will probably lose his job at the circus and its all because his "slender" wife no longer loves him since she has grown so fat.

Other columns transformed for the stage involve the tales of two murderers and their hanging (on stage)—one a wife killer and the other a black labor organizer charged with committing a murder during a labor riot.

The Play is a fine introduction to Hecht's style and creative mind and his love for story telling. After leaving Chicago, Hecht wrote several novels, the plays mentioned earlier and over 70 screenplays, including Scarface, Gunga Din, Notorious, Kiss of Death and portions of Gone with the Wind. Returning often for visits to Chicago and the scenes of his "1001 Afternoons in Chicago," he died of a heart attack in 1964.

28

Eli Wiesel and *Night*

About thirty years ago I had the opportunity to meet Eli Wiesel during a weekend he spent in Chicago for a program sponsored by the Midwest Region of the American Jewish Congress, which I believe was his first public program in Chicago. This was years before he received the 1986 Nobel Peace Prize and before his fame made him undoubtedly the most heroic figure to emerge from the Holocaust. A group of us spent an afternoon of discussions with him on the Sabbath and spent the evening singing Hebrew and Yiddish songs at one of our member's house. On the following day, Wiesel spoke to a large audience at a downtown hotel, culminating in a panel discussion with several young people on matters of concern to them. The question of Israeli policy with respect to the then newly occupied territories won by Israel after the Six-Day War, was a "hot" discussion item. It is hard to believe that now, thirty years later, that topic is still with us.

We have seen and heard Wiesel many times in Chicago since this first public visit. The last time was on Wednesday, April 17, 2002, when he appeared as the guest of the City of Chicago at the Harold Washington Library Center before a crowd of approximately 600 people. He was in Chicago to mark a celebration culminating the "One Book, One Chicago" selection of Wiesel's book *Night* by

Mayor Richard Daly. The "One Book, One Chicago" project had begun the prior year with a successful presentation of the novel *To Kill a Mockingbird*. Since its selection by the City, *Night* has sold thousands of additional copies and is being read and studied in schools throughout the area.

Night was written in serial form in Yiddish in France by Wiesel ten years after his liberation from Auschwitz. It is a small book, originally published in 1955, and details in simple words the horror that descended on a young 15 year old Wiesel when he was sent to a death camp with his entire immediate family. Without any warning, his mother and sister quickly were separated from him at the camp, and he was left only with his father, a deeply religious man. The book's power is in the words, just as Wiesel's oral presentations are powered by the simplicity and the power of his language.

Wiesel began his program by noting that he had just returned from Israel after a week's trip and "never have I seen Israel so sad" he said. He then stated, "With all my heart and soul I denounce the suicide killers. This should stop, then many things will be possible."

Wiesel spoke for nearly an hour. He stressed repeatedly that the Holocaust was "unique," and he dealt with his continuous struggle to comprehend the Nazi's attempt to exterminate the entire Jewish people, no matter of what sex or age. There have been many atrocities in our time, as in Serbia and Africa, he said, but none compared to the Holocaust. In somewhat of a departure of his usual calm manner, his voice rose in anger when he was asked about American policy during the Holocaust, chastising President Roosevelt for refusing a safe haven for the liner "The St. Louis" with its 1,000 Jewish refugees and the refusal of Roosevelt to order the bombing of the "rails" leading from Hungary to Auschwitz when it was obvious that Hitler's policy was to transport Jews by trains to the death camps.

He concluded his remarks with this message for the audience. We must preserve our stories and memory of the horror that was done to our people. Survivors of the Holocaust must "bear witness" as to the evil that they endured and this can be done best by writing. "Write your stories" Wiesel urged, and that is how you can memorialize our history. It was a fitting conclusion for this great man. It is also a meaningful message to all of us in the Chicago Jewish Historical Society. Wiesel's message not only applies to the "Holocaust" but should inspire each of us to write. Write your story and that of your family to preserve it for future generations.

29

Dr. Erika Fromm, Famed Psychologist

Several years ago I taped an oral history of Dr. Erika Fromm, a friend of my wife and myself, who passed away on May 26, 2003, at her home in Chicago's Hyde Park neighborhood at the age of 93. Erika was an emeritus professor of psychology at the University of Chicago and a world renowned expert on the use of hypnosis in therapy. I interviewed her at her summer home in Michiana, Michigan, a few minute walk away from my home there.

She recounted for me a brief history of her life. She was born Erika Oppenheimer in Frankfurt, Germany in 1909 into an observant Jewish family. From a young age, she aspired to an academic career. With Nazism on the rise, she managed to earn a doctorate from the University of Frankfurt while it was still possible for a Jew to do so. She recalled her fear and the discrimination suffered by her family as Hitler rose to power. She fled, with her younger brother, to Holland in 1934 where she stayed until her fiancé, Paul Fromm, managed to obtain visas. They immigrated to the United States in 1938. Incidentally, her husband was a cousin of the psychoanalyst Erik Fromm. People often assumed Erika was a blood relative of Erik Fromm, but she was not. Paul Fromm and his family were well-known wine merchants in Germany, and though the Nazis confiscated their business, Paul was able to create a prosperous wine enterprise in Chicago. He was also a lover of music and created the Fromm Music Foundation which continues to support contemporary American composers by annually commissioning new works and subsidizing premiere performances. He was also an avid baseball (White Sox) fan and spent many afternoons in the country listening to the games, which Erika said was not particularly her main interest. Paul Fromm died in 1987.

Erika's parents did not escape the Holocaust, though her sister and several brothers did. One of her siblings lives in Israel, one in Germany and one in California.

From her position as a research associate at the University of Chicago, she joined the faculty of its psychology department. During this period she was a prodigious writer on dream interpretations and signal work on the use of hypnosis as an effective tool to help people with their psychological problems. Being no different than most, I quickly offered myself as a possible patient for such treatment—but somehow we did not manage to do it, and now it is too late. Erika published her last book in the year 2000, quite an accomplishment for a person 90 years of age. But though she was not well and beset by tragedy (her daughter died in a home accident), she was already in contact with a publisher about another book.

We discussed her Jewish heritage for a bit, and Erika was keenly aware of her Jewish roots. Her family name was Oppenheimer and she told me that she could trace the family lineage in Germany back to the sixteenth century, but her German experience had left her with a bitterness against Germans and she herself said she was a "non-believer." We did not pursue that subject. As we ended the interview, she handed me an article she had written in 1992 for a German magazine which had wanted to translate from English into German one of her books, and for which she did not give her consent. The article is titled "Personal Feelings of a Nazi Refugee: Why I do not want to be Honored by Germans."

Erika Fromm was interred at a private graveside funeral at Oakwood Cemetery on Chicago's South Side.

30

Albert Einstein: The "Undesirable Alien"

The 2003 "Einstein" Exhibition at the Field Museum was the subject of an interesting article published in the January 2, 2004 *Chicago Tribune* "McCarthy-era witch hunters did not spare Einstein" by Staff Reporter Ron Grossman.

Grossman writes that prior to America's entry into World War II, "shrill voices" had called for the deportation of Albert Einstein, a Jewish refugee from Nazi Germany, as an "undesirable alien" because of a fanatical fear that his pacifism and alleged suspicious acts made him a security risk.

Grossman writes "In 1939, Einstein learned that German scientists were poised to translate his $E=MC^2$ equation into a deadly military reality. So he urged FDR to beat Hitler to the atomic bomb." The *Tribune* reporter continues that if "a small but persistent group of super patriots—whose ranks included J. Edgar Hoover—had had their way Einstein might not have remained in the United States to share his fears with Roosevelt. No other scientist so captured the popular imagination that a president would feel obliged to heed his advice."

The letter referred to was on display in the Hebrew University's traveling exhibit on the life of Albert Einstein that made a popular, months-long stop at the Field Museum. Einstein's letter warned

Roosevelt of the possible development of an atomic bomb by the Nazis and prompted Roosevelt to order the Manhattan Project to "harness the atom's power" and beat Germany to the punch. Also on display were copies of a few of the thousands of pages of surveillance reports the F.B.I. kept on Einstein, who was considered a "security risk," and prevented from participating in our nation's wartime scientific efforts beyond some mathematical work for the U.S. Navy.

It was without doubt a shameful conduct by Hoover and American "super patriots" in their behavior toward Einstein and culminated years later in the so-called "McCarthy Era" of harassment and discrimination of anyone suspected of "suspicious" anti-American activities.

Another famous Jew, Martin Kamen, was also the victim of this type of harassment by American authorities, including the F.B.I., Hoover and the military establishment. Martin Kamen was abruptly fired from his scientific position, later named by the Congressional UnAmerican Activities Committee and then vilified in the headlines of the same Chicago newspaper that recently carried a sympathetic story about Einstein's ordeal, except that in the Kamen story the *Tribune* itself was part of the "super patriot" group. We call attention to the *Chicago Tribune* of this sorry tale of its behavior as a reminder that one must remember history in all of its phases. The *Tribune* reporter was correct in reminding us of the "Einstein" incident, but he might also have recalled the conduct of the *Chicago Tribune* in the years prior to and during the McCarthy era.

31

Chicago Jewish Philanthropists

Chicago Jewish Philanthropists played a leading role in reestablishing and reorganizing the University of Chicago in the last decade of the nineteenth century. Thereafter the University seemed to have had a special attraction for Jewish scholars as well as donors.

In the 1930s, as Hitler threatened the very existence of Jewish life in Germany, many German Jews sought refuge in America. Among them were renowned intellectuals. United States law at the time allowed entry to immigrants only if they could obtain an affidavit of support (or job) from an American institution or citizen.

In this context, the University of Chicago, under its then President Robert Maynard Hutchins, was of special assistance. A number of leading German émigrés were invited to join the faculty. Among them were Professor Hans Morgenthau (Political Science), Professor Max Rheinstein (Law), Professor Bruno Bettelheim (Psychology), Hannah Arendt (Political Science), and Professor Leo Strauss (Philosophy).

A later émigré was Professor Karl Joachim Weintraub, who came to Chicago after the end of World War II. He was born in Darmstadt, Germany in 1924. His parents, a Jewish father and a Gentile mother, sent him to the Netherlands for safety when the Nazis came to power. When the Germans invaded the Netherlands, he was hidden by a Quaker family and his life was saved. At The University of Chicago he earned his undergraduate, master's and doctoral degrees, and in 1954 began teaching in The University College while still a graduate student. The U of C was to be his home for 60 years. He died on March 25, 2004.

On April 21, 2004, the respected writer and commentator Andrew Patner, a student of Professor Weintraub offered a memorial tribute on his WFMT radio program, *Critics' Choice with Andrew Patner.*

"One of his great influences at Chicago was his own teacher and fellow refugee, Christian W. Mackauer, whose selfless devotion to the Western Civilization course that Weintraub went on to embody became a model for the younger man. . . .

When, for a complex number of reasons, younger faculty members lost interest in teaching his beloved course, Mr. Weintraub uncharacteristically became something of a fighter. Recalling his time as a hidden child and adolescent, he told several people, 'I had enough of life without civilization.' Illness took him from his own teaching soon after... His life was one filled with the search for understanding, and his death is surely the end of an era."

A memorial service was held on Friday, April 30, 2004 at Rockefeller Memorial Chapel. Karl J. Weintraub's long devotion to the University of Chicago, and the intellectual contributions of other émigrés who found refuge there, indicate that the early Chicago Jewish community leaders made a good investment.

32

A Three Generation Visit to Israel

In the summer of 2004, my wife, Chaya, and I went on a trip to Israel, accompanying one of my daughters, Miriam, and her husband, Mark, and their three children (my grandchildren) Jonah, Emma, and Talia, at the time—ages nine, seven and three, respectively. Our visit was for a three week stay, and Miriam and Mark (and their clan), who are professors at SUNY University at Albany, were staying on for the summer months for a sabbatical at Ben Gurion University, in Beer Sheva in the Negev/the South of Israel.

My first trip to Israel had been in 1952 when I participated in a year long work and study program at Maàle Hachamisha, a kibbutz located in the Judean Hills near Jerusalem above the Arab village of Abu Gosh. After that initial stay, I had been in Israel many times, often with my family, the last time being about ten years ago.

Returning to Israel this time was somewhat different since, for the first time, we were traveling with grandchildren in Israel. Given the seemingly grave political and security situation, we did not expect what we encountered. Since our stay did not include visits to Gaza or West Bank settlements, I do not have any first hand observations as to the situation in those areas, but in the rest of Israel that we visited, and we drove over 1400 kilometers going from North to South and around, the country looked superb, with an enormous amount of construction in many areas. Throughout the country, the roads have been rebuilt and are in extraordinarily good condition. Except for the appearance of the "Fence" (or Wall as some call it) in some areas, little military personnel or equipment was visible. But this report is not meant to be commentary on Israel's geography or economy, nevertheless I do say to our members, family and friends, visit Israel—it is a marvelous vehicle with which to identify with the people of Israel. As part of this identification, I would like to share with you the places we saw and the people we met.

We stayed at a guest house in Kibbutz Sasa, located above Safed, near the Lebanese border. It was established by a group of young *chalutzim* (pioneers) from America after the War of Independence in 1948. When we visited, by sheer coincidence, there was a reunion of *vatikim*, original settlers. Among them were a number of Chicagoans, some who are still living on the kibbutz and others who had come from Chicago and other places. One of them was our close friend Lynn, a woman who almost 40 years ago lived with us in Chicago and helped take care of our children while she was studying. She had taken our belief in Zionism seriously and had immigrated to Israel. She now has five grown children, some already married, and is a teacher and writer. It was a reunion on a grand scale as we toured together in Northern Israel. The Waterfalls at the Banyas, the Hula Valley and of course, Lake Kinneret where, if you go to the right place, you can walk on water.

Lynn's kibbutz, Sasa, now faces the problem that is pervasive among the kibbutz community. The old communal way of life is undergoing privatization of both its social and economic life. Though at Sasa, those who desire, can still eat in the community hall, most members eat in their own houses. Children sleep at home but Sasa schools are still communal, and its economy is prosperous today as its factories have been converted to the manufacture and assembly of security and other defense items for delivery to the

"Coalition" forces fighting in Iraq. All this may be rather ironic, since Sasa was built by young idealists, with leftist leanings, who yearned for peace, not war. With that said, Sasa also has an excellent school for young children from surrounding areas and has a vibrant cultural life (including tennis courts).

We left Lynn and drove South to Maàle HaHamisha. This was the kibbutz where I lived for over a year fifty years ago. I had come there after a stay at a Zionist summer camp in New York, and had met David Ron and his wife Batya, who were "shlichim" (teachers and counselors) from Israel. It was David who persuaded me to come to his kibbutz after I finished Law School in 1952. My stay at the kibbutz was a most gratifying experience, a second home for me, and when my year was up, I left the kibbutz with sadness. My friend, David, a teacher at the kibbutz, passed away twenty-five years later from multiple sclerosis. I kept in infrequent touch with Batya over the years, but when I wrote her of my visit this year, she replied immediately, and I was delighted to hear that she was still active and well. A one-time director of the guesthouse at the kibbutz, she was still working there, now part-time, at the new hotel that had been erected at the edge of the kibbutz. Needless to say, when we arrived at Maàle HaHamisha, we were given penthouse rooms and there were chocolates in our rooms from Batya. Later that evening, we walked down from the Hotel a short distance to the kibbutz proper, where Batya was waiting for us near her house. Now over 80 years of age, she stood as erect as ever, still lovely in all ways, which age could not change. It was a moving moment for Chaya and myself. The next day we returned to Batya's house for coffee and a Viennese "tart" with her and her son, Shlome, who is "Mazkir" (Secretary) of the kibbutz. We discussed problems affecting the kibbutz, that is also undergoing "privatization;" the community dining hall is closed and there is now a shop on the kibbutz where people can purchase necessities for eating at home. Soon, Shlomo tells us, each member of the kibbutz will own his own home and some land. The hotel and other enterprises will be owned by a legal entity, such as a co-op arrangement in which the members will share. Later, Chaya and I took an oral history of Batya.

She was born in Vienna, and at the last moment in 1938, was able to escape as the Nazis occupied Austria. Most of her family was trapped in Austria and later perished in the Holocaust. Batya, through the efforts of Zionist organizations, was able to reach Palestine and sent to a kibbutz near Tel Aviv. There she met David Ron, who was a young Chalutz from Poland. She and David were married, and by the time I met them in 1952 in Chicago, had two young sons. My grandchildren were excited by many of the things that they saw at the kibbutz, including a large swimming pool and play area, but the biggest thrill was to witness hundreds of cows coming in from the fields to be milked by machines, while standing and feeding on a huge moving "carousel" contraption. The next day, after dinner at an Arab restaurant at Abu Gosh, we left and continued our trip southward to the guest house at kibbutz Ein Gedi.

Ein Gedi abuts the Dead Sea and a park and spa located there, which if you like salt water and mud baths will make you very happy. I myself was happier with our tram ride up Masada, the great fortress of Roman times, which was of great meaning to all of us when we talked to our grandchildren of its meaning to all Jewish people and Israel.

From the Dead Sea area we drove to our final destination—Beer Sheva and the Ben Gurion University. Miriam and Mark had rented a house in Omer, a suburb on the outskirts of the city and quite miraculously we found that their neighbors were an elderly couple from Antwerp, Belgium whom we had last seen in 1969. We now met them again, and they showed us picture albums of Chaya when she was a student-teacher with him in Antwerp over 50 years ago. But that is another story, and another coincidence which often occurs in Israel. Near the end of our trip a friend of Mark's asked us to accompany him for a visit to Lakia, a Bedouin settlement situated in the Negev, about twenty kilometers from Beer Sheva. The Bedouins are traditionally a nomadic people, living in clans, of Islamic faith but considered friendly to Israel. The Negev has been their private campground over the years, but now with more and more Israelis moving into the Negev, the Bedouins are under pressure to settle in permanent villages of their own and claim ownership of the land where they settle. As we came to Lakia we met several young women who told us that they are the leaders of an organization called the "Association for Improvement of Women's Status in Lakia." Two young Bedouin women dressed in colorful long dresses, the leaders of this organization explained to us that women's traditional role in their society is caring for their men and animals in a nomadic setting, where young women were not permitted to have a basic education of reading and writing. With the transition to an urban life, women could no longer contribute to the economic well-being of their family and so this Association was formed to improve children's education and literacy for women generally, and other objectives to improve the rights of women. To do this and to provide employment for women, they had established an operation for weaving and embroidery by Bedouin women for decorating dresses, carpets and other objects, all in many colors and patterns. Over 160 women are said to be employed by the Association, though there is opposition to their efforts by the male hierarchy in the Bedouin establishment. At this point, however, they appear to have the approval of the Israeli government, and they receive some financial support from European sources. We were served some Turkish coffee as they presented some of their wares to us. We bought some objects and left enchanted by these inspired, lovely and hard-working young women, beset by problems, both internal and external, that will take great effort and patience to overcome.

We concluded our stay in Israel after staying for several days in Beer Sheva, now a bustling city with Ben Gurion University as its hub. On a Saturday night we joined some friends and scores of

Israeli, for a weekly demonstration calling for the withdrawal of Israel from the Gaza and West Bank settlements. It was a peaceful demonstration, and the vehicles and Israelis who passed by the demonstrators at best seemed to agree with the demonstrators, and if not, they were indifferent to their presence.

So that is a glimpse of our trip to Israel. Inspiring and enchanting as ever—with problems that will continue to challenge and necessitate difficult solutions.

33

How to Kiss a Catholic Priest

I don't recall ever having the opportunity to embrace and kiss a Catholic priest before my trip to Northern Italy in the first week of September 2004. There, in the foothills of the Maritime Alps, on the border between France and Italy, I had that opportunity, and I acted on it. The Priest in question was the Sacerdotte, Don Francesco Brondello, who at the age of 84 had managed, with his assistants, to bring himself to the beginning of a mountain path that 61 years earlier Jews, fleeing from the Nazi hordes invading Italy after its capitulation in November 1943, were crossing to safety in the mountains of Italy. The scene was almost surrealistic; we were high enough so that clouds surrounded us and goats and cows with bells around their necks grazed in the distance while mountain streams could be heard rushing by. And there sat the Priest, his ever-friendly smile on his face, welcoming my wife, Chaya, and my children and grandchildren, and Chaya's sister Gitta and her similar clan (and several friends, together with relatives, from Israel, America and Germany who had come to join us).

We also met with the family of Andreina Blue, who had helped Chaya's mother and her daughters by supplying food and a haven in the caves of the mountains. Andreina was one of the many resisters to the Nazis when they invaded Northern Italy. She is deceased now but her daughter, Anna, though 78 years of age, is hale and hearty, as are Anna's daughter and granddaughter and their spouses, who were also with us.

Don Francesco himself was in his early twenties when the Germans invaded Italy in September 1943 after the capitulation of Italy to the Allies. He was a flamboyant figure, an excellent skier who could been seen streaming across the Alps with his black cape and red hair flapping in the wind. With Chaya's great efforts in securing the necessary papers, he had recently been awarded the title of "Righteous Among the Nations" by Yad Vashem in Jerusalem for his courageous deeds during the War. He had been part of the Italian resistance, much like Primo Levi, the famous author who fought in the same mountains. As assistant Priest to the Parish of Valdieri, the young Priest had helped Jewish people by bringing them winter clothes, providing false papers and financial aid. One story he related to us was how he delivered 84 letters for Jews in Italy across the mountains to their families still remaining in France. He was caught by the Nazis, imprisoned for a time and tortured (and he has the scars to prove it). Many of the Jews who crossed the mountains from France into Italy were later captured by the Nazis and sent to their death in Auschwitz in cattle cars, some of which are now on exhibit in a nearby railroad station.

The trek up the mountain was difficult. I walked about half way up, but others continued, and a few reached the top. From there, this path then descends into France, whence the Jews originally came in 1943. This walk of remembrance is now an annual event. Next year, the walk will be in reverse and start in France.

The story of this miraculous escape is not mine and should be told by my wife, which I am assured she will do in the form of a book in the near future. Let me add, however, that the story of Jewish survival is universal, and if you happen to visit Italy, plan a few days up near the city of Cuneo and town of Valdieri. There are still small communities of Jews, who survived the Holocaust, and they will welcome you. The sprit of Don Francesco Brondello seems to permeate the area, and I found nothing but welcome for Jews from these people who helped other human beings, risking their own lives in doing so. That is why I was glad to embrace this Priest with all my gratitude. He had helped to save the life of my wife, the mother of my children, and grandmother of my grandchildren. Without him, none of them might be alive today.

34

Hecht and Levin

I had the pleasure and satisfaction of making a presentation on Wednesday, February 9, 2005, at Newberry Library based on several essays from my book *Looking Backward: True Stories from Chicago's Jewish Past*. The central theme of the presentation was Ben Hecht's and Meyer Levin's heroic efforts to help rescue European Jewry in their acts and writings before, during and after the Second World War. Adele Hast and Bev Chubat read excerpts from my book.

Upon reflection, another theme appeared in the lives of these two authors, namely American concepts of free speech as it applied to obscenity, confidentiality, and blacklisting. The following are First Amendment issues that arose in both their lives:

In 1923, Ben Hecht lost his job with the *Chicago Daily News* because his novel *Fantazius Mallare* was considered to be obscene by the US Postal Service. By today's legal standards, the book would not violate the law and would have been protected by the Bill of Rights.

In 1947 Hecht's films, books and other works were banned in the British Empire. In April of that year, in Palestine, the British Army had hanged four members of the Irgun in Akko Prison, and the Irgun had retaliated by hanging two British soldiers. In May,

Hecht placed a fiercely worded ad in major newspapers lauding the Irgun's action. He was blacklisted in Hollywood, and like other shunned writers in the McCarthy era, worked under an assumed name. His First Amendment rights may have been violated by the American movie companies, but Hecht never chose to litigate.

In 1959, Meyer Levin and his publisher, Simon & Schuster, and the movie studio 20th Century Fox, were sued by Nathan Leopold in Illinois courts to prohibit the marketing of *Compulsion*, the book and movie based on the Loeb and Leopold murder case. Nathan Leopold's main contention was that his right to privacy was violated by Meyer Levin's work. Levin countered that the United States Constitution's guarantee of free speech protected his work.

In my book *Looking Backward: True Stories from Chicago's Jewish Past*, I discuss the case in detail. On April 15, 1964, Judge Thomas E. Kluczynski ruled in favor of Leopold, writing that both the book and movie "constitute a classic case of an invasion of the rights of privacy." Levin appealed and eventually won. I quote him: "... Costly and protracted, the battle provided a precedent for literary freedom" After Leopold appealed, the case eventually went before the Illinois Supreme court, where, on May 27, 1970, Judge Daniel P. Ward issued an opinion upholding Levin's victory.

35

Aaron Director, University of Chicago Free Market Economist

On June 14, 2005, I attended a University of Chicago Law School Symposium in memory of Aaron Director, a celebrated University of Chicago "free-market economist" who helped unite the fields of law and economics. He died on September 11, 2004, in Los Angeles at the age of 102.

While Director published sparingly and was almost unknown outside of his intellectual circle, he was well known for his "free market" teachings at the University of Chicago, influencing many students and colleagues, including the jurists Robert H. Bork and Richard Posner. He also founded, in 1958, with Nobel laureate Ronald H. Coase, the influential "Journal of Law and Economics." I was fortunate to be a student in his class at the Law School for two years in the early 1950s in a course on Law and Economics which he taught in collaboration with Edward H. Levi, later to become Attorney General of the United States. Director was Jewish and a brother-in-law of the University's well-known "free market" advocate, Milton Friedman.

Director was born in 1901 in Charterisk, in the Ukraine, and came to the United States in 1914 with his mother and siblings to join his father, who had preceded them in their migration to the

United States, seeking a new life here after his business failed. A brilliant student from the beginning of his education, Director received a scholarship to Yale University in 1921, from which he graduated in 1924. He was a "liberal" in his early years, went on trips to Europe and returned to obtain a teaching position at the Portland Labor College.

From there, at the suggestion of a friend, he came to Chicago in 1927 for his graduate studies. At the University, he met Paul Douglas, an economist, who offered him a fellowship and he became Douglas' assistant in his studies of the labor market. He was a student of and worked with Douglas for several years. (Douglas later became a leading liberal politician in Chicago and became an alderman and a Congressman from the Hyde Park area and later Senator from Illinois.)

In 1930 Director was appointed an instructor of Economics. He now came to know Frank Knight and Henry Simons, economists at the University and many other economists, a number of whom became Noble prize winners.

In 1946 at the age of 45, Director began to teach at the University of Chicago Law School. Now began his relationship with Edward Levi, who split the "Law and Economics" course between them, Levi teaching it for four days and Director for one. It was said that Director used his one day to show that Levi's legal analysis "simply would not stand up." Director's teachings led to the creation of the Volker Fund, which gave fellowships to exceptional students for the study of economics and its affect on the enforcement of the anti-trust laws. One of the students who later became quite famous for his views was Justice Robert H. Bork. By 1950, when I attended this class, Director argued for a pro-business line to reduce taxes on large corporations and eliminate tariff protections. He became the leader of the "Chicago School of Economics" which reached its greatest influence with the ascendancy of Ronald Reagan to the Presidency. To say that Director was no longer the "liberal" of his earlier years is an understatement. But to this writer, despite his conclusions and "free market" views, he is remembered as a brilliant teacher with an ability for incisive insights.

In my senior year, I received a very low grade on my final examination in his class. Since I disagreed with the grade and since I thought I had understood all of his perplexing questions, I availed myself of an appeal process to see the Professor to discuss my exam. He received me courteously and said he remembered my paper and that I received a low grade because he could not read my writing, which was illegible to him. I requested he let me read my answers to him, which he granted, and without a word, he raised the grade on my exam from 68 (C-) to 78 (A-). This I accepted with thanks and told him that I thought he taught a great course.

36

Italy 2005: Victory Celebration

In September 2004 our family traveled to Northern Italy to honor the priest, Don Franceso Brondello, with the State of Israel's designation, "Righteous Among the Nations," and to honor the family of Andreina Blua, who had helped save the lives of my wife, Chaya, then a young girl, her mother, Hannah, and her sister, Gitta, and other Jews who had fled over the Maritime Alps from Occupied France to Italy in 1943. The trip culminated in our family's attempt to cross the Alps from the Italian side (Colle de le Ciriegia) into France.

Chaya was invited to return to participate in the next commemoration scheduled for September, 2005. The organizers were Sandro Cappellaro and Alberto Cavaglion, Historian of the Institute of the Resistance and Contemporaneous Social Political Issues in Northern Italy. They received us with warm hospitality, picking us up from the airport at Nice and driving through the mountains to Saluzzo, where Sandro and his wife, Piera, put us up in a private apartment above theirs. We were hosted every night by other families of Christian friends who are dedicated to the study of the history of the persecutions of Jews and the Resistance of their compatriots to the Nazis from 1943-1944. We greatly enjoyed 5-course meals of Northern Italian cooking amid lively political discussions.

Saluzzo is a medieval town, nearly 1000 years old, located on a road that started in ancient Rome and led across the Maritime Alps. Though there is a restored synagogue in the old Jewish Ghetto of Saluzzo that dates back to the fifteenth century, there are no Jews living there now. Those who had not been able to flee or go into hiding by 1944 were killed in Auschwitz.

The history of this part of Northern Italy is highly complicated. There were many small towns around Saluzzo in which Jews lived and maintained synagogues dating back to the year 1000. But there are no functioning Jewish communities in this area, except for those in the cities of Turin and Milan.

We learned from our discussions that there were some Italians who helped Jews and others who were fascists and vicious anti-Semites. The people who were our hosts were descendants of resistance fighters. They tended to make the saving of Jews part of their contributions to the resistance to the Nazis.

On Friday, September 9, our daughter, Judy, her husband, Steve, and our grandchildren, Miko and Tema, joined us, almost unexpectedly, to help us relive an historic occasion. That evening in a gathering of approximately one hundred guests including historians, the mayors of three surrounding towns, university students, descendants of resistance fighters and others, Chaya gave a talk of her experiences in Italy and France during the War, and Judy spoke about the Shoah legacy as a member of the third generation after the Shoah. A serious discussion ensued that culminated in the question posed by a young Italian student: "Why should we remember the Holocaust?" The evening ended with an informal dinner prepared by this most dedicated group of friends, to which Chaya and I contributed our share of wines and dessert. Fireworks and some resounding choral singing topped it off.

On September 10, our Italian friends drove with us to the small town of St. Martin Vesubie in France, where 1000 Jews fled the Nazis on the day of the Italian Armistice of September 8, 1943, and crossed the French Alps into Italy. Chaya and her family were among them.

Then, on September 11 in the early morning, a large group of people drove up to the gathering point called the Madona, the same place from where the Jews fled in 1943. From there, those who felt they were able to do so proceeded to scale the Colle de Finestre, a mountain with large treacherous rocks. After a long climb of over two hours and accompanied by cold, torrential rain and hail, Miko, Tema, Judy and Steve reached the top and joined an Italian group that had come up through Italy. Chaya managed to reach the top with difficulty. Nevertheless she spoke at the top about her experience in 1943, about the September 11 New York disaster, and about Katrina. "When government fails," she said, "individuals have to act according to their conscience!"

After returning from the mountaintop we attended a rally in a driving rainstorm in St. Martin where Yad Vashem honored three families who had hidden a number of Jews during the War. That rally ended with the singing of the Hatikvah and the Marseillaise, something poignant when thinking about the Vichy France of 1942–1943 and its anti-Semitic policies.

The next day, our last in Europe, we took a hike to the neighboring village of Venacon. I was determined to scale a mountain, even if I did not do it the day before. And with the encouragement of my daughter and grandchildren I climbed a difficult path to a place called the "End of the World" from where we had a magnificent view of a huge valley. There were many small houses in that valley and I wondered how many Jews had tried to escape to this place for whom this indeed had been the End of the World.

37

How the Son of Ulysses S. Grant Helped a Galitzianer

I saw the intriguing headline "How the Son of Ulysses S. Grant Helped a Galitzianer" while I was perusing a recent issue of *The Galitzianer*, a quarterly newsletter of Gesher Galicia (Bridge to Galicia), the special interest group for Jewish families from Galicia, a province of the former Austro-Hungarian Empire. My wife, Chaya, and I belong to this genealogical society.

The "Galitzianer" headline referred to Charles Pitzele, who had lived in Chicago. The story was written by Ben Weinstock of New York. I sent Mr. Weinstock an e-mail expressing my interest in his article. He replied that he was interested in the story because it concerned a family whose surname was Pitzele, of which he thought he was a descendant.

The Pitzele family had been one of the wealthiest families in Galicia. Descendents of the Pitzeles had immigrated to America in the 19th century. The story noted that some of the Pitzele family came to Chicago in the 1870s, including Charles Pitzele. He had returned to Galicia for a visit. He went to Krakow and other places in Galicia and was arrested for not having done his required service in the Austrian military. Charles was rescued from imprisonment only with the intervention of the son of an American President Ulysses S. Grant.

Mr. Weinstock had spent over a decade researching the Pitzele family in America. He scoured the records of the New York City Public Library and there search engines led him to Illinois and Chicago. The Grant story appeared in an edition of the *Chicago Tribune* dated November 23, 1890, reporting that a case had just come to light involving the arrest of an American by the Austrian government. The person named was Charles Pitzele, who resided in Chicago and was a naturalized citizen. He was arrested by a Polish officer on the grounds that he had left Galicia without serving in the Austrian army. He was "thrown in jail" and kept there for nearly a week.

Charles Pitzele appealed to American Minister Frederick Dent Grant, the son of Ulysses S. Grant, who was for a number of years the United States minister to Austria-Hungary. On the direct intervention of Frederick Grant, Pitzele was released, but not before he was compelled to pawn the jewelry of his wife and sister in order to post a bond for his release. The story later appeared in the *Congressional Record* as well as many American newspapers, including, as indicated above, the *Chicago Tribune*.

Mr. Weinstock informed me that he had found no living Pitzeles who were his relatives. I checked Chicago sources and found only one Pitzele family listed in the phone records, but they knew nothing of their ancestors and they pronounced their name differently than the Yiddish pronunciation. We also discovered that members of the Pitzele family, including Charles, had lived in Chicago on the far south side and were involved in various business activities and some local politics. Norman Schwartz, the Society's expert on Jewish cemeteries, also discovered that Charles and many members of the family were interred in the Ohave Shalom Mariampole section of the Oak Woods Cemetery on the south side of Chicago.

President Grant's son, Frederick, became a hero with the Jewish community for his efforts to help the Pitzele family. Frederick was the first of the Grant children, born in 1850. He followed in his father's footsteps, into the Army (U.S. Grant had performed poorly as a West Point cadet, and Fred's record at the Academy was even worse), and then politics. President Benjamin Harrison appointed him United States minister to the Austro-Hungarian Empire, and he served from 1890 to 1897. He was appointed New York City Commissioner of Police in 1897, succeeding Theodore Roosevelt. That same year, Grant's Tomb, in New York's Riverside Park, was dedicated. It is the resting place of President and Mrs. Grant, and the largest mausoleum in North America. Frederick Grant commanded troops in the Phillippines during the Spanish-American War in 1898. He died in 1912.

38

A German-Jewish Dialogue

My wife, Chaya, and I attended an evening meeting on June 22, 2006, at the Self-Help Home, 908 W. Argyle, which is a retirement home originally established on the South side of Chicago in 1950 for Jewish refugees who had escaped Nazi Germany. With the passage of over half a century, the Home today is greatly expanded. Its current facility houses one hundred-fifty Jewish residents, many of whom are neither refugees nor from Germany.

We were invited to the meeting by Mr. Gerald Franks, a member of our Society, who co-chaired the evening event. It was sponsored by the American Jewish Committee and the German Consulate General as part of their ongoing series of German-Jewish dialogues. The chairman of the meeting was Deputy Consul General Peter Primus.

The principal guests were seven German high school students ranging in age from thirteen to seventeen years, as well as several of their teachers. They were introduced by David Sperling, Professor at Northeastern University, and a distant relative of Julius Rosenwald, the famous Chicago Jewish philanthropist, was one of the speakers at the meeting. The audience itself consisted primarily of residents of the Self-Help Home, many of whom had come from Germany.

Sperling explained that the German youngsters were visiting various cities in the United States to learn about American Jewry as part of a special project promoted by their hometown in Germany dealing with the history of the Jews of this town before and during World War II and the tragedy that befell the Jews. This town is called Bŭnde and is located in Northwestern Germany, near the City of Hanover. Today it has a population of about 45,000, none of whom are Jews. In November, 1938, at the time of *Kristallnacht*, there were about 250 Jews remaining in Bŭnde, many others had managed to escape from Germany. Of those remaining, only three were survivors of the Holocaust. The students from Bŭnde had taken oral histories about their town's Jews and had participated in a "weeping stones" project—inscribing stones, each with a murdered Jew's name on it, and displaying them in the town. One of the teachers, and some of the students, gave short talks about their perceptions of what had occurred in Germany and what they had learned about Jewish life. It was a very moving experience, winding up with one student singing a beautiful lullaby in Yiddish.

This presentation was followed by a question and comment period, which was quite difficult. Some of the elderly members of the audience wanted to know from the students what they had done, particularly in their own families to learn of their family's role during the persecution of the Jews. Most answered quite honestly that their grandparents and parents did not want to talk about it at all—or claimed they knew nothing about what happened to the Jews. This brought about sharp retorts from some in the audience who wanted the students to become more involved. It brought tears to some of the students. One student (the one who sang our Yiddish lullaby), when pushed on the question about what he was doing with his family, answered "I am learning how to convert to Judaism." This brought applause from the audience and basically ended this immensely honest interchange with these German youngsters. I might also add that the questions asked of the youngsters which I mentioned above, do not necessarily represent the view of many others in the audience who felt that the German students were doing a good thing in German Jewish relationships.

As a finale, it is interesting to note that Professor Sperling reminded the audience that Bŭnde was the birthplace of the father of Julius Rosenwald who left Bŭnde in 1854 to immigrate to America, where Julius Rosenwald was born.

A few days after the "German Jewish Dialog" event, I attended a signing program at Newberry Library where Peter M. Ascali, a member of our Society and a grandson of Julius Rosenwald, introduced his new book: *Julius Rosenwald: The Man Who Built Sears, Roebuck and Advanced the Cause of Black Education in the American South*. The book contains a fine biography of the life of Julius Rosenwald, and his great achievements in the business world, and the immense contributions he made in the world of philanthropy.